'There are not that many topics that have consistent application in all types of coaching. Optimising energy available to clients to fulfil their tasks is one of them. I would say that this topic is nowadays more often on the table than any of us as coaches would wish it to be. Why? Because this topic is as elusive as energy itself. However, Viv Chitty has taken this big challenge and put it at the centre of her exploration. She does this methodically and intelligently, unravelling complex concepts and offering practical ideas in a way that is clear and immediately applicable for our complex practice. A very important read for coaches and coaching supervisors.'

Prof Tatiana Bachkirova, *Professor of Coaching Psychology,*
Oxford Brookes University

'You know that thing that to grow asparagus, you had to start 3 years ago? Well, Viv Chitty has done more years than that of research on energy, including an award-winning Masters degree. The result is we have this very serious, hugely important, and deeply research-based book, made available to us *right* when we need it, when the enduring pandemic has exhausted the world. It's written for executive coaches, and will be required reading for that profession, but it should be core reading for medics, students, and anyone in business. Or health. Or the pro bono sector. Or government – particularly government.'

Catherine Devitt, *CEO, Meyler Campbell, Executive Coach*
former Director of People and Development at Breakthrough
Breastcancer Care and Director of HR HBOS Canada

'This rigorously researched book is a gift to practitioners, clients and organisations; it addresses, in detail, the often ignored territory of human energy in the context of the workplace.

Viv Chitty asserts that having optimal energy is essential for high performance and she is right. Many aspects of energy are thoroughly addressed here: physiological, emotional and cognitive including stress – all fundamentally important in life and in business.

Bringing appropriate attention to our energy levels has never been more necessary and *Coaching for Optimal Energy: A Guide for Executive Coaches* could not be more timely. I am delighted that the result of such important research is now available to coaches and their clients.'

Edna Murdoch, *Founder/Director of the*
Coaching Supervision Academy

Coaching for Optimal Energy

A completely new way of considering energy in executive coaching, the concept of Optimal Energy® is based on original research. This fresh insight and its application is a fundamental new approach for use in executive coaching.

Suboptimal energy levels in senior executives, although rarely considered, can negatively impact efficacy, feelings, behaviour and self-awareness both at work and in coaching sessions. But what is optimal energy? This needs to be addressed by executive coaches, but how? *Coaching for Optimal Energy: A Guide for Executive Coaches* answers these questions and challenges previous thinking on the subject. Written for executive coaches, and appropriate for anyone who works with people, for the first time in coaching literature the book gives a research-based definition of the concept of energy and examines how energy manifests in clients, analyses the influences on energy and offers clear guidance and practical ideas for addressing energy with clients.

This is an essential new resource for coaches and other practitioners who want to effectively address energy and enable clients to take action to optimise their energy in their daily lives.

Viv Chitty is a highly experienced executive coach, with over 20 years' experience, a coach supervisor and has a background in consultancy. Amongst other qualifications in psychology and counselling she holds an MA in Coaching and Mentoring. Viv runs a coaching consultancy which works with senior people in a wide variety of sectors. She is passionate about working with senior clients who have multiple challenges to face.

Coaching for Optimal Energy

A Guide for Executive Coaches

Viv Chitty

Second edition

ISBN: 978-1-7393395-0-0 (pbk)
ISBN: 978-1-7393395-1-7 (ebk)

First published in 2023 by Routledge.
This second edition published in 2023.

British Library Cataloguing-in-Publication Data
A catalogue record for this book is available from the British Library

Book design by The Unbelievable Book
Layout by Sally Osborn
Interior graphics by Deb Marcy

VCA Publishing
Viv Chitty Associates, Unit 97415, PO Box 6945, London W1A 6US
https://vivchittyassociates.co.uk

Contents

List of Figures

Acknowledgements

The author acknowledges and expresses her gratitude to the following for permission to reproduce their work in this book:

Judy Brown for the poem 'Fire' from Brown, J. (2008) *A leader's guide to reflective practice*. Victoria, BC: Trafford Publishing.

Where my research is concerned, I would like to thank my tutor/supervisor, Dr Adrian Myers at Oxford Brookes University, for his support and challenge whilst I worked on the dissertation and my research participants, fellow executive coaches who kindly took time out of their busy lives for the interviews. I would like to give a big thank you to Dr Daniel Jenkinson and Dr Jane Jenkinson for writing their input on the medical impacts on energy. Where both the dissertation and book production is concerned, Deb Marcy, my virtual PA, has been patiently by my side throughout the whole process and has produced some great diagrams! My family and friends have also supported and encouraged me throughout; including the publisher Tom Drake-Lee whose comments I greatly appreciate. And lastly, but so very important, thank you to my dear late Mum whose response, despite being so very poorly, to my saying that I was writing a book was such a beaming smile that I could never give up.

Preface

WOULD YOU KNOW HOW TO ADDRESS energy levels in your clients if you thought it necessary? A few years ago I didn't.

I started executive coaching in 1998 and in the following years developed my practice coaching senior executives in a range of organisations. Over the years I became increasingly aware of differing energy levels in my clients: some had appropriate energy levels to cope well with their working life and others were exhibiting, and describing, problematic energy levels and were at times struggling to meet the demands being made on them. Their energy both impacted their performance at work, their relationships in and out of work and, in my opinion, their ability to put into action what they had decided to do as a result of their coaching.

So I decided to look into the subject of 'energy'. But I found very little around apart from self-help books. I embarked on a journey hunting for research on the topic and found very little of use. Meanwhile I continued to wonder whether I should be addressing the concept of energy directly with clients. I began to read practitioner literature which addressed energy and discovered the concept of 'energy management' described by the psychologist Dr Jim Loehr and the journalist Tony Schwartz whose argument is that energy, not time, is fundamental for high performance (Loehr and Schwartz, 2003). But I still felt frustrated: what was the answer to my question regarding what I could do as a coach?

At the same time I started to work with several senior clients, for whom energy levels seemed to be an issue, and began to actively address their energy in sessions. These interventions were well received and deemed helpful. I wrote a coaching programme for my clients for whom it was relevant. I also used these strategies myself and found them effective at a time of life when many demands were being made of me.

However, my interventions were not based on academic research. I found the meaning of 'energy', in the little literature that there was, to be implied neither explained nor based on research. I struggled to define energy personally too, initially coming up with 'our capacity to do, perform and act', yet I realised that this required further work. Nevertheless 'energy' seemed to be something that I and others intuitively understood, for example, I suggest that most could understand what was meant by someone saying 'I've got no energy today!' I started to wonder if it was just me who saw the influence that energy levels had on clients. Were other executive coaches addressing energy levels in coaching and, if so, how? Did they think it relevant and important?

I decided that I wanted to research the subject further, properly. In the end I embarked on a Masters in Coaching and Mentoring Practice at Oxford Brookes University in order to do so. The resultant dissertation was entitled 'An exploration of energy in the context of executive coaching: what it means, what is witnessed and how, if relevant, it might be addressed'. Using the research method 'Conceptual Encounter' (De Rivera, 1981) I interviewed peers, other executive coaches, and each interview furthered the design of the concept and models, so the models I present in this book were developed in collaboration with other practitioners. The dissertation was awarded the APECS prize for the best dissertation on an executive coaching or supervision topic: maybe I was on to something.

One of the aims of the Conceptual Encounter research method is for the results to inform practice, enable practitioners to recognise the experience, in this case of energy in clients, and to be able to respond in a suitable way (De Rivera, 1981). I pondered what I might do to share the findings with other coaches and this book is the end result. Given that client energy, until now, has not been researched in the field of coaching, it is hoped that the book will fill some of the gaps in existing knowledge and encourage, and inform, debate and practice. The book provides insight into the concept of human energy in the context of the workplace and the potential influences. It aims to help the reader become more able to recognise manifestations of energy in clients, the impact on their performance and provide practical insight into how this could be addressed with clients once it has been assessed whether it is appropriate to do so.

As much as is possible the content is based on academic, peer-reviewed research. This was important to me, I wanted the book to reflect more than my ideas, and also believe that it might be useful for fellow coaches to have some research to back up their work with more sceptical clients who may need some information about what really can work.

Those of you who have carried out research will know that when you do so you have to be very specific about your research boundaries, so I chose to carry out the research in the context of executive coaching, it being my field of work. This book is based on my research findings, hence the focus is on executive coaching. However, it is my belief that what I have written is applicable to all types of coaching, maybe with the odd tweak here and there, to coach supervision and for practitioners not in the coaching 'world' who may want to address energy with their clients: such as counsellors, therapists and those in General Practice. I do believe that most of us working with other human beings in one-to-one or group work may at some point notice that someone's energy levels are impacting them in some way. This work also applies to the coach's own energy: we too are surrounded by the same influences, need to be aware of our own energy and take appropriate action. The book does not consider therapeutic and healing practices such as energy psychotherapy (a highly complex therapy which works with energy centres and meridians), reiki and chakra work which all should be provided by trained, and in some cases very highly trained, practitioners. These interventions may well be appropriate for some clients to address energy but they are not my area of expertise.

I have tried to be generic in my approach to writing this book not following one particular theoretical perspective, school of psychological thinking or psychotherapeutic influence. I hope that putting in some points, for example from the field of neuroscience, will be of use to the reader. I have also not entered into debates about who is right where there are disputes in the literature because this would have taken over the book! This may mean that a deep dive into the thinking in some of the areas has not been possible, but, hopefully the journey this book takes the reader on will offer some useful insights for most.

The contents

Chapter 1 explores the concept of energy, what it is, and how it may manifest in executive coaching clients thus broadening out the conceptualisation by detailing the influence a client's energy can have on how they feel and behave. The presence of optimal energy in clients reflects a positive concept: energy being a resource which enables people to act and perform. This chapter challenges previous thinking, moving away from the linear model of low/bad versus high/good energy. The many influences on energy are explored in Chapter 2.

Chapter 3 considers why it is important to address client energy and whether it is the executive coach's role to do so. I argue that two of the overarching roles of an executive coach are to enable clients to perform better and to become more aware of themselves and that this involves considering what might get in the way of, and what might enhance, their performance: energy levels do both.

The rest of the book explores what executive coaches can do to address a client's energy levels and the barriers to them doing so. In Chapter 4 it is proposed that the coach can enable the client to increase their awareness of their energy levels, how they manifest and the impact, and together create a holistic, self-directed 'package' of interventions rather than just use one energy management strategy as previously researched. This package would be tailored to the client's specific needs, relating to differing energy levels and could include interventions to calm, maintain, restore and/or release energy. Such a package of interventions would be designed following assessment of the current situation and the gathering of information.

In Chapters 5, 6 and 7, I explore how energy can be addressed, this is partly based on what has been previously researched in fields other than coaching with the addition of more in-depth ways of working. Chapter 5 outlines how physical energy can be addressed, Chapter 6 considers working with emotions and Chapter 7 examines working with cognitive influences on energy. The aim of this section is not to dictate how to coach, as Nancy Kline mentioned in the context of her recent book, it is a description not a prescription (Kline, 2020), nor do I intend to present yet another coaching model, but to lay out the options and some pointers for fellow coaches to take from as they wish.

Implications

This has implications for senior clients. If they are able to maintain and regain optimal energy levels, their well-being and subsequent impact on colleagues can be improved as well as their efficacy and ability to sustain performance. This may in turn influence organisational performance and sustainability. Another implication is that if senior people learn how to manage their energy and take this aspect of self-care seriously they will be good role models and hopefully encourage others in their organisation to do so as well, and back support programmes to support the health and well-being of staff whatever label is given to the initiative. I am left wondering whether we, executive coaches, are doing our clients a disservice if we do not consciously assess whether their energy levels are appropriate for what they are trying to achieve and help them to address this, whether by enabling them to sustain them at their current level or to become more appropriate. This book is the result of years of thinking and research. I hope that you see that it comes from my passion to work with my clients in a way that is of service to them. I saw a gap in my knowledge and coaching 'tool kit' and sought to fill it. But this is just the beginning, there is so much more to find out. There is a need for further research into what methods of addressing energy are most effective and in what combination, the underlying physiology and how long the effects of certain interventions last. I look forward to hearing from colleagues about what they think and discover.

References

De Rivera, J. (1981) *Conceptual encounter: A method for the exploration of human experience*. Washington, DC: University Press of America.

Kline, N. (2020) *The promise that changes everything: I won't interrupt you*. London: Penguin Random House.

Loehr, J. and Schwartz, T. (2003) *The power of full engagement: Managing energy, not time, is the key to high performance and personal renewal*. New York: Free Press.

1

The concept of energy and how it manifests in executive coaching

MOST OF US MAY USE THE WORD 'ENERGY' in our everyday language but what does it actually mean? This chapter offers a research-based consideration of the concept of energy before developing the understanding of energy further by detailing how it manifests in our work as executive coaches with our senior clients.

Defining energy: the literature

When I looked deeper into the subject of 'energy' I found no research in the coaching literature and therefore broadened the scope of review to include organisational and management studies, social sciences and psychology. However, the more I searched the wider literature the more surprised I became about how little human energy in the context of work has been researched, defined and written about. Even in the energy management research papers and self-help books the meaning of energy was largely implied, not explained, nor based on research. And it wasn't just me scraping the bottom of the 'research barrel'. Academics also wrote that they found this to be the case despite 'energy' being a pervading concept 'that is often mentioned in relation to physical and mental health and fitness, in Western philosophy and theory' (Schippers and Hogenes, 2011, p. 193).

Instead of a commonly used definition, certain indicators of energy and being energised are widely used in the literature: 'vigour'; 'vitality' and 'engagement'. 'Vigour' has been described as 'high levels of energy and mental resilience' at work (Schaufeli and Bakker, 2004, p. 295), an active and positive concept, which is a similar concept to 'vitality', 'a positive feeling of aliveness and energy' (Kinnunen *et al.*, 2015, p. 1079). Engagement, a concept from the field of positive psychology, has been described as a 'positive, fulfilling, work-related state of mind that is characterised by vigour, dedication, and absorption' (Schaufeli and Bakker, 2004, p. 295). In addition, indicators are used which relate to a lack of energy such as 'exhaustion' described as 'feelings of overstrain, tiredness and fatigue' (Kinnunen *et al.*, 2015, p. 1079) and 'fatigue' which is described as feeling 'depleted, tired and sluggish' (Fritz, Lam and Spreitzer, 2011, p. 28).

The original four types of energy identified in much-quoted literature

As I continued to search the literature I read the much-quoted book *The Power of Full Engagement* (Loehr and Schwartz, 2003) which suggests that there are four different types of energy: physical; mental; emotional and spiritual. But subsequent research has challenged this, arguing that 'energy is not mental, social or spiritual per se' and that these categories are influences on energy rather than types of energy (Quinn, Spreitzer and Lam, 2012, p. 342). Influences will be explored in-depth in Chapter 2.

The proposed concept of 'energy'

Two interrelated components

Rather than there being four different types of energy, it has been proposed that energy is a resource made up of two interrelated components, as illustrated in Figure 1.1, physical energy and energetic activation (Quinn, Spreitzer and Lam, 2012).

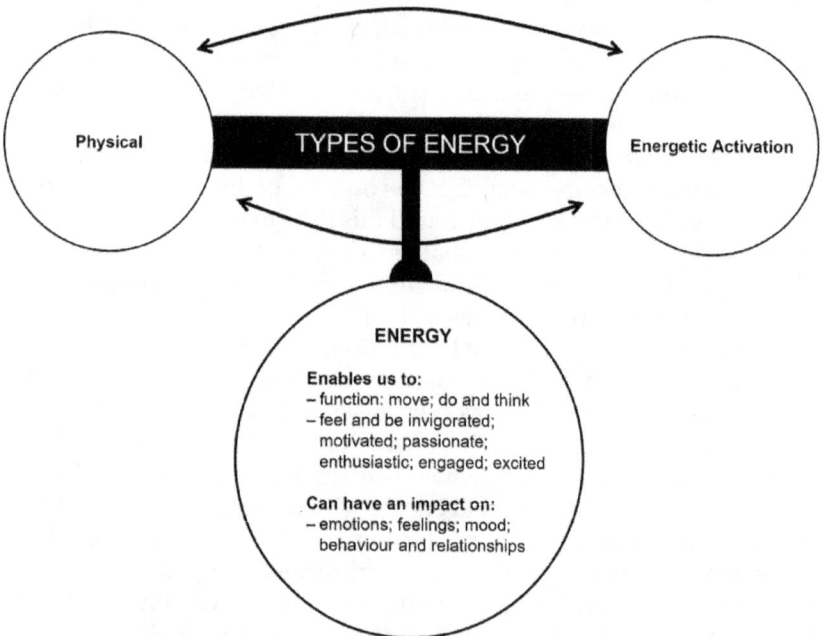

Figure 1.1 The concept of energy

Physical energy

Physical energy derived from nutrition, oxygen and hydration is suggested to be what enables individuals to 'move, to do and to think' (Quinn, Spreitzer and Lam, 2012, p. 341) and is depleted by 'intentional' actions, such as movement, and 'unintentional actions', such as brain activity, breathing and unconscious thought.

Energetic activation

Energetic activation is described as the degree to which people feel energised by their emotions (Quinn, Spreitzer and Lam, 2012). It has also been described as motivational energy (Brown, Kingsley and Paterson, 2015). Energetic activation is experienced as vitality and positive arousal (Parker and Gerbasi, 2016; Quinn, Spreitzer and Lam, 2012) and is a source passion, motivation, engagement and excitement. From the perspective of neuroscience, it is thought that positive energising will result from the experience of 'attachment' emotions (Brown and Dzendrowskyj, 2018), often called 'positive' emotions, that allow people to thrive (Lanz and Brown, 2020). This will be explored further in Chapter 2.

It is important to note that there is a distinction between energetic activation, which comes from positive emotions, and 'tense activation' (Thayer, 1989) which motivates people to respond in perceived threat situations and is linked to what are referred to as 'negative emotions' or 'escape/avoidance' emotions (Brown and Dzendrowskyj, 2018) which are proposed to result in a 'survive' way of being. What I will refer to as 'survive' emotions from now on do not enhance work-related performance and functioning for a number of reasons which I will explore in greater depth in Chapter 2.

The distinction between physical energy and energetic activation is useful to explain, for example, why one might have sufficient physiological resources for action in the form of hydration and nutrition, and be fit, but experience depleted energy and motivation because of negative emotional and cognitive influences on energetic activation.

The relationship between physical energy and energetic activation

It is interesting to consider how physical energy and energetic activation are related. For example, one may feel depleted in physical energy due to a lack of sleep, poor nutrition or dehydration and this in turn may lead to feeling stressed and worried, for example, about how one is going to handle the day. This makes absolute sense if we believe that the mind and body are inextricably linked together (Gailliot and Baumeister, 2007; Claxton, 2015). I remember a friend saying to me when I was being woken twice every night by my baby, "You'll feel worse if you worry about how you will feel the next day, it will lead to more stress, just go with it and you might be pleasantly surprised". In other words, fretting in the middle of the night about the tiredness that may result from disturbed sleep can mean that you are hit at both the physical and emotional level, both the lack of sleep and the fear and anxiety, when actually you may not end up feeling as awful as you fear.

Energy: a resource that can be both replenished and liberated

In much of the research into human energy, energy is referred to as a 'resource' or a 'fuel': something that makes it possible for a person to function well in situations they face and tasks they need to undertake, with drive, ambition and motivation. There are differing schools of thought in the literature with regard to whether energy is a 'scarce' resource, a finite tank of energy, which can be depleted and needs to be managed to allow recovery and sustainability, in other words, the tank refilling (Parker and Gerbasi, 2016; Schulz, Bloom and Kinnunen, 2017) or an 'abundant', infinite, resource which can be 'released' or 'liberated', for example, by the interest that people have in their work and colleagues that they mix with (Cross, Baker and Parker, 2003). However, it may be too simplistic to consider energy as either scarce or abundant, a finite or infinite tank: it may be both. One may be energised by activities and relationships but also require rest and recuperation.

How energy manifests in the coaching context: three categories

The rest of this chapter focuses on what executive coaches may witness with regard to client energy in sessions. What I write is based on my own experience and that of other executive coaches, my research partners whose observations are quoted throughout this book (all the quotes in this chapter are reproduced with their permission). Being aware of how the concept of 'energy' may manifest in sessions can further the ability of executive coaches to recognise the influence of energy on client behaviour, levels of engagement and feelings, and to work with this.

Three categories of energy witnessed: a challenge to past descriptions

This chapter presents a conceptualisation which challenges the portrayal of energy in related literature, and in general conversation, of 'low' energy (a negative concept indicating tiredness, a lack of excitement and motivation) versus 'high' energy (a positive and constructive concept). I propose that the previous linear representation is both a simplistic and an inaccurate portrayal of client energy and offer a more complex conceptualisation: that there are three overall categories of energy witnessed, optimal, depleted and inappropriately high energy and that this is dynamic and fluid, in that the energy a client exhibits can change even within a session. Unlike the linear representation with high energy as a positive concept, this conceptualisation suggests that having high energy may not always be positive but can be problematic, not constructive nor enable the building of relationships. And that 'low' energy may be positive, for example when one is contemplative, and is not necessarily a negative state to be in (as we know, introverted people may come across as having low energy but can be great leaders). A comparison of both conceptualisations is offered in Figure 1.2. In other words, I suggest that some people performing at optimal energy levels may be exhibiting low, for example, calm energy and so-called high energy in clients may be far from optimal.

The detail: how coaches witness these types of energy in sessions

The coaches I interviewed in my research were able to describe at length how they witnessed client energy in sessions. What I write below is based on our collective experience supported by related research where it was available.

Optimal energy

Whether the level of personal energy is 'optimal' or 'appropriate' is dependent on the individual and what they are trying to achieve, their circumstances and the people involved. How Optimal Energy® is witnessed in sessions can be grouped into two main clusters:

- Firstly, clients coming across as truly engaged, motivated, in 'flow', passionate, enthusiastic and driven
- Secondly, the client being able to concentrate (in a sustained way) with sharp, focused attention, thus being 'present' in the session

In addition, clients who are optimally energised in a session could come across as:

- Considered, with the conversation having a regulated pace
- Optimistic
- Happy with their lot and what they are doing
- Able to see the bigger picture
- And this may manifest physically, for example, with the client having straight posture and a 'spring in their step'

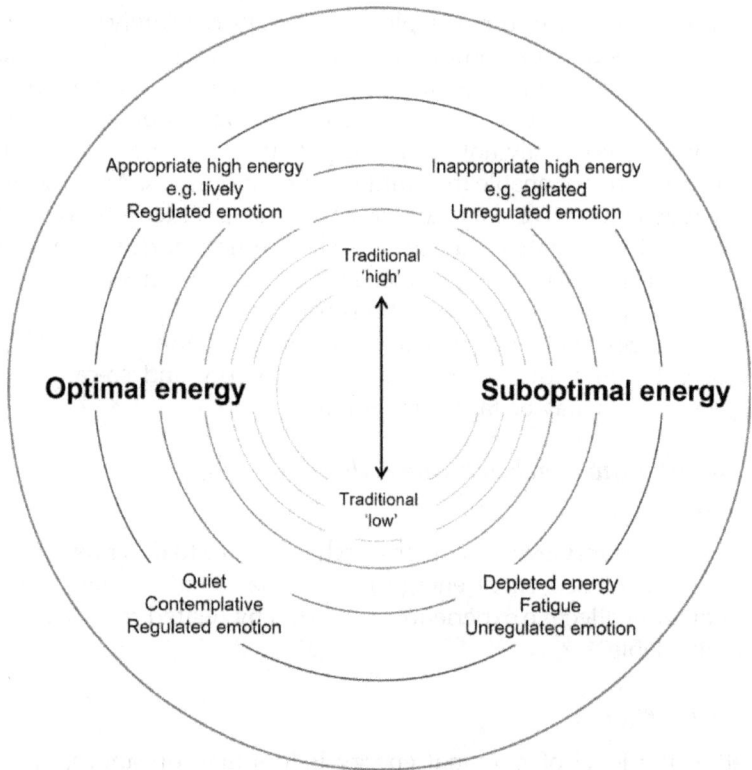

Figure 1.2 Traditional categorising of energy versus the new conceptualisation

> *People I work with who say, "I'm inspired"; "I'm loving what I do"; "I'm feeling so enthusiastic"; "Oh, I feel better"; "I can see the bigger picture". It's that conversation where somebody has put some pre-thought into it. It has a more regulated pace, even though the conversation might obviously not remain entirely focused, but it is considered. We are able to say: okay, so this is the thing that it would be useful to work on today.*

> *People who are well slept, well hydrated and have got energy for their day. And so I think that comes down to the basic stuff … people who clearly go to the gym, get up and do a bit of exercise in the morning, have slept and get themselves to bed on time. That transmits very visibly at a physical level.*

Depleted energy

Depleted energy can manifest in a whole range of ways, from clients who seem less lively than usual and not seeming like their 'normal self' to more serious behaviours indicative of depression or being in a fragile state of some sort. A negative state of depleted energy is described in the literature as 'exhaustion'; 'feelings of overstrain, tiredness and fatigue' (Kinnunen *et al.*, 2015, p. 1079), 'emotional exhaustion' (Schaufeli and Bakker, 2004; Parker *et al.*, 2017) (see the section on Burnout) and 'fatigue'. Clients can come across as weary and lacking enthusiasm with cognitive manifestations such as:

- Having a lack of focus including wandering attention
- Not being able to reflect, step back and think
- Lacking interest, maybe seeming as if they can't be bothered
- Avoiding conflict, being less courageous

The client may exhibit or talk about emotions and feelings such as:

- Fear
- Frustration
- Sadness
- Feeling lost and/or overwhelmed
- Anxiety
- Concern about their level of tiredness and worrying that this may get worse and impact their well-being

This can be witnessed audibly and visually with the client having:

- A slow pace of speech
- A lower tone of voice
- Shortness of breath
- A tense body
- A lack of eye contact

Depleted energy can impact client performance, both in coaching sessions and at work (where the latter is concerned see Chapter 3). For example, within sessions a client's pace may slow down and they can come across as lackadaisical, very slow in their thinking, idea generation and ability to consider how they can put intention into action. This could mirror how they are in other situations, for example, a client who comes across like this in a coaching session may well seem like this in meetings and be less effective as a result.

I think there are some fairly obvious signs: peoples' body language; the way they breathe; the way they hold their face; their facial expression. You hear it in the voice tone as well, when people are looking tired, feeling tired. (An illustration being when) we need to gain clarity on an action plan and it just feels like we're dragging our feet. The pace slows down. So there are lots of small indications.

When energy is depleted it can lead to a client feeling emotionally wrung out, that is the point where insanity speaks because they have nothing left to be rational with [...] no emotional buffer left to absorb the next hit and the next hit actually damages.

Inappropriate high energy

The third category of energy witnessed in coaching is inappropriate high energy which makes functioning appropriately more difficult for the client. Inappropriate high energy can be witnessed as:

- A lack of focus, with clients being 'all over the place', which may get in the way of both concentration and dialogue
- Anger which may be perceived as 'attacking', the person being more in 'fight' mode than 'flight'
- Agitation and abrasive behaviour
- Being overly enthused or overly focused

This client had been very aggressive with me (in previous sessions). I went in to see him to tell him that I wasn't going to work with him any more. But he looked different and I asked him if something had happened. (I found out that) he was actually very down. I hadn't realised it. And that's why he'd been vicious with me.

Inappropriate high energy may result from emotions such as anger, but can also result from overexcitement, overstimulation and overworking of the mind (Childre and Rozman, 2005).

Lack of focus: you get this complete splurge of information. I was with a guy yesterday who was tapping on the table the whole time. I reflected back to him that he was tapping and also moving his head around. He said, 'You know, I'm doing this all the time'. I could tell his whole head was just a 'buzz'. And it wasn't useful. It was absolutely getting in the way and so I had to work quite hard to get him centred and focused.

I see the young bucks come in with boundless amounts of energy: thinking, 'I'm going to go and change the world' but having no idea of what they're up against. And sometimes I guess that that boundless enthusiasm works and sometimes they just end up as a red stain on a wall as they run headlong into it.

Figure 1.3 summarises how these three categories of energy are witnessed in executive coaching sessions. It is important to stress that this is a summary and is not intended to be used as a diagnostic tool because obviously people will exhibit energy in different ways, for example, we may witness highly extroverted displays of energy when

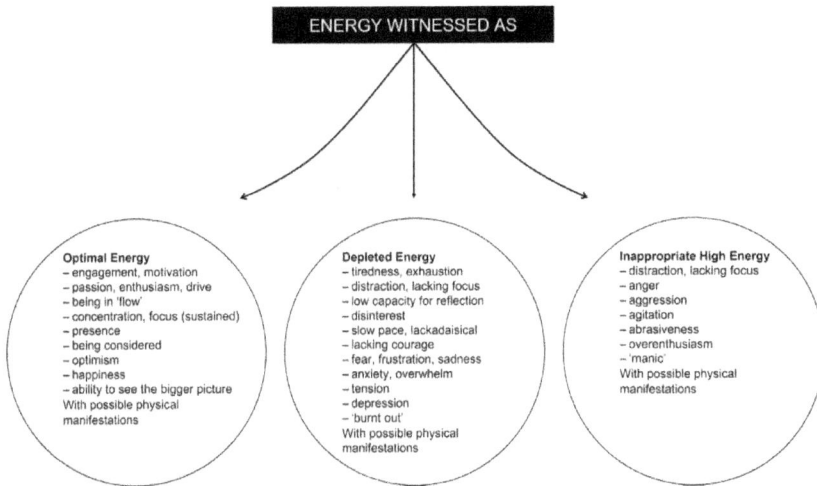

Figure 1.3 How energy levels are witnessed: the three categories

clients are speaking with great passion, whereas others may be hugely driven but talking in a much calmer way. However this is very useful information to gather when working with the client which can be fed back and worked with if appropriate.

When depleted energy or inappropriate high energy may be indicative of something serious

Depleted energy: an indicator of depression, burnout and trauma

Depleted energy may be indicative of the client being in a fragile psychological state such as depression or being close to 'burnout'. It can also be symptomatic of a reaction to trauma.

Depleted energy is one of the main indicators of depression along with a range of components which can range in severity and length of time experienced, such as: persistent low mood with a loss of interest and enjoyment; having too much or too little sleep; appetite changes; feeling guilty or self-critical and having poor concentration (MacKinnon, 2018). This may be accompanied by a sense of hopelessness and having suicidal thoughts. There is also a condition called 'subsyndromal depression' where depressive symptoms are present but do not lead to significant impairment (Mufson *et al.*, 2011, p. 5). The BMJ guidelines (MacKinnon, 2018) stress that medical diagnosis is essential, therefore if a cluster of these symptoms were present it would be important for the coach to take this to supervision and encourage the client to seek medical advice or make the referral if necessary, as detailed in Chapter 4.

> *Having been criticised quite heavily* (he exhibited) *frustration, hurt and demoralisation, depression I think. And my whole sense of this guy is that his energy is so fragile … he's so fragile. I don't think he's sleeping.*

Significantly depleted energy in the form of emotional exhaustion, which refers to the draining of emotional energy and feeling of chronic fatigue, along with a sense of helplessness, can also be indicative of burnout (Maslach, Schaufeli and Leiter 2001; Quinn, Spreitzer and Lam, 2012; Maslach and Leiter, 2016), which again would warrant referral. Burnout is not a description purely of tiredness, it is a serious psychological state which develops over time. We need to be careful about the terminology we use and care needs to be taken not to confuse burnout and/or emotional exhaustion with fatigue or tiredness which employees may experience more commonly. Symptoms of burnout can include depersonalisation; detachment from emotions and feelings; feelings of cynicism; detachment from and a lack of interest in work, feeling that one has to do tasks rather than being driven by seeing their value and thinking that one is ineffective and not accomplishing anything (Maslach, Schaufeli and Leiter, 2001; Maslach and Leiter, 2016; Riethof *et al.*, 2019). Although there are debates about cause and definition it is widely accepted that in its later stages burnout is characterised by overwhelming and total emotional exhaustion accompanied by thinking that one is helpless to address how one is feeling and being unable to achieve high levels of energetic activation in any context (Quinn, Spreitzer and Lam, 2012). The individual may suffer from physical weakness and difficulty sleeping. There are many causes of burnout such as demanding work conditions and tasks and prolonged stress. It is interesting to note that there is a powerful argument for seeing burnout not as an illness or disorder, but the 'body doing its very best to protect us by creating the conditions under which it might have a chance to recover' (Lanz and Brown, 2020, p. 117).

Reactions to trauma are physical and psychological and may include depleted energy in some form, sometimes referred to as 'hypo-arousal', particularly when strong emotional, cognitive and physical reactions are experienced. Trauma can result from directly experiencing or witnessing a traumatic event, both individually and collectively if the trauma impacts a whole society or group of people. Such events, both one-off or multiple, are defined as ones which involve 'actual or threatened death, serious injury, or threats to the physical integrity of the self or others that result in intense fear or helplessness' (American Psychiatric Association, 1994). We cannot predict how people will react nor what they need to do to cope. When I led the workplace consultancy for the National Office of Victim Support a key message was that people may be fine, they may not, do not assume. But whatever their reaction, it is a normal reaction. And the effects can last from days to years. A recent traumatic experience may also reignite the thoughts relating to, and impact of, past trauma. Where depleted energy is concerned, the client may:

- Be very fatigued
- Be emotionally numb, in a state of shock
- Feel that they are lacking a meaningful purpose in life that could motivate them to invest energy in daily tasks and pursue goals (Flannery, 2012)
- Be socially disengaged

Trauma can also sometimes result in Post-Traumatic Stress Disorder (PTSD) and, whether this diagnosis has been made or not, the stress response can be triggered long after the event and there can be problems with flashbacks (reliving aspects of the event), difficulties sleeping, self-blame, avoidance and anxiety to name a few.

Inappropriate high energy: an indicator of manic episodes, early-stage burnout and trauma

As with depleted energy, inappropriate high energy may be indicative of a number of serious conditions, for example, it could be symptomatic of a manic episode due to bipolar spectrum disorder or the early stages of burnout and it is also another traumatic stress reaction.

Bipolar spectrum disorder, a psychiatric diagnosis, is a recurrent or chronic mood state characterised by a wide range of symptoms including unusually elevated or irritable moods and overly high energy levels (Hirschfeld *et al.*, 2000). In addition, the person may exhibit 'disruptive symptoms of distractibility, indiscretions, grandiosity, flight of ideas, hyperactivity, decreased need for sleep, and talkativeness' (Selvaraj, 2021) alternating with phases of depression. Coaches need to be aware of the condition and the shorter lasting and less severe condition of hypomania, and understand when referral is necessary for professional diagnosis (see the section on referral in Chapter 4).

Going back to burnout, but in the context of inappropriate high energy, it is interesting to note that four stages of burnout have been identified and a tendency towards over-commitment has been noted during the earliest stages. As a result people can become overloaded because they have unrealistic expectations about their capabilities, taking on a lot of tasks to prove that they are fine professionally or to impress others, whilst disregarding their own needs. This is characterised by a positivity that all is well, which has been referred to as 'naïve enthusiasm', along with denial of the negative consequences (Riethof *et al.*, 2019). Could it be that some of our clients who are exhibiting inappropriate high energy are actually in the early stages of

Physical

TYPES OF ENERGY

Energetic Activation

ENERGY

Enables us to:
– function: move; do and think
– feel and be invigorated;
  motivated; passionate;
  enthusiastic; engaged; excited

Can have an impact on:
– emotions; feelings; mood;
  behaviour and relationships

ENERGY WITNESSED AS

Optimal Energy
– engagement, motivation
– passion, enthusiasm, drive
– being in 'flow'
– concentration, focus (sustained)
– presence
– being considered
– optimism
– happiness
– ability to see the bigger picture
With possible physical
manifestations

Depleted Energy
– tiredness, exhaustion
– distraction, lacking focus
– low capacity for reflection
– disinterest
– slow pace, lackadaisical
– lacking courage
– fear, frustration, sadness
– anxiety, overwhelm
– tension
– depression
– 'burnt out'
With possible physical
manifestations

Inappropriate High Energy
– distraction, lacking focus
– anger
– aggression
– agitation
– abrasiveness
– overenthusiasm
– 'manic'
With possible physical
manifestations

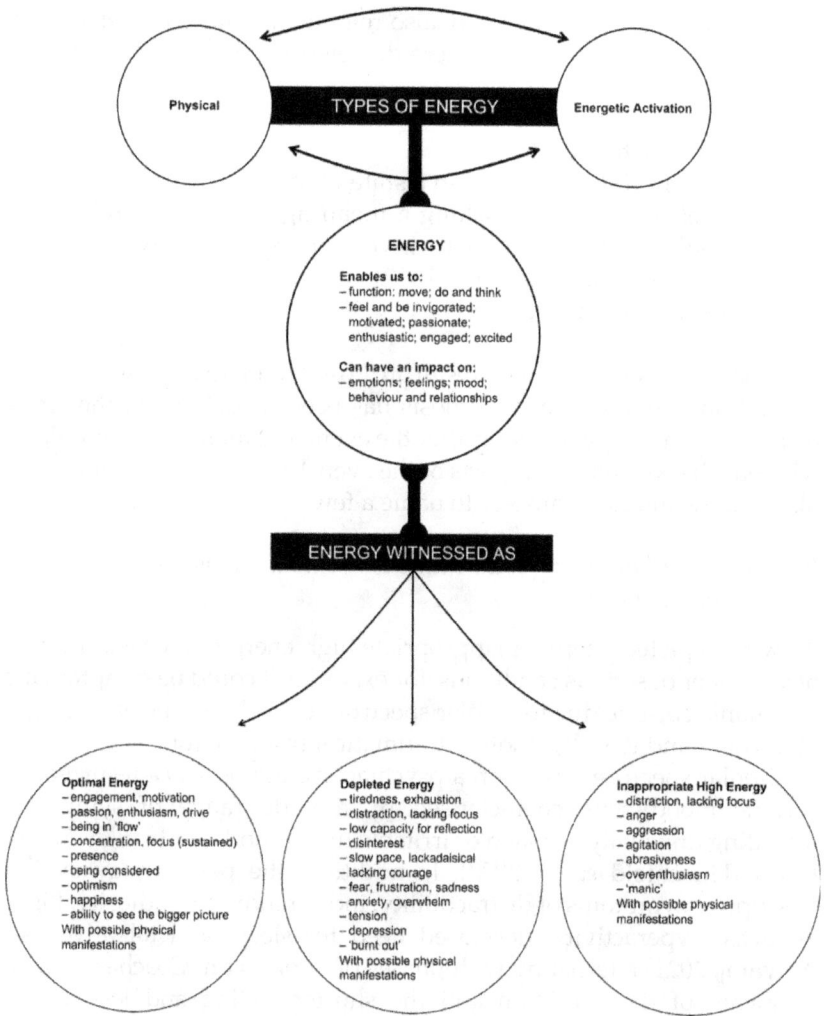

Figure 1.4 The concept of energy in the context of executive coaching

burnout, desperately trying to show to themselves and others that they are fine and are coping?

Another way in which a person may react to trauma in relation to energy is that the client may be highly energised due to heightened arousal, 'hyper-arousal', which can result in them being hyper-alert or hypervigilant, very sensitive to sound, touch and visual cues. After a traumatic event hyper-arousal is useful in that it can give people access to a lot of energy for a short period of time, maybe until they feel that the threat has passed, but it may continue for longer and not be as useful. In addition, the resultant stress response may include a reduced ability to control one's behavioural state and difficulty in both listening and being able to extract meaning, which may be interpreted as lacking interest or being inappropriately energised.

Energy: a summary

Human energy is derived from both physical resources and energetic activation. It enables us to function (move, do and think), feel invigorated and act with eagerness and motivation, influencing emotions, feelings, behaviour, relationships with, and impact on, others. In coaching sessions the executive coach can witness client energy levels as being optimal, depleted and inappropriately high and this can change even within a session. This summary is detailed in Figure 1.4.

Understanding the concept of 'energy' and how it may manifest can enable executive coaches to be aware of their clients' energy levels in sessions and recognise the influence of energy on client behaviour, levels of engagement and feelings. Furthermore, having this knowledge will allow coaches to inform their clients about the concept and help them to understand their energy levels and their impact.

References

American Psychiatric Association (1994) *Diagnostic criteria from DSM-IV*. Washington, DC: American Psychiatric Association.

Brown, P.T. and Dzendrowskyj, T. (2018) 'Sorting out an emotional muddle', *Developing Leaders*, **29**(Spring), pp. 26–31. London: IEDP: Available at: https://iedp.cld.bz/Developing-Leaders-issue-29-Spring-20181/26

Brown, P., Kingsley J. and Paterson, S. (2015) *The fear-free organization*. London: Kogan Page.

Childre, D. and Rozman, D. (2005) *Transforming stress: The HeartMath solution for relieving worry, fatigue and tension*. Oakland: New Harbinger Publications.

Claxton, G.L. (2015) *Intelligence in the flesh: Why your mind needs your body much more than it thinks*. New Haven CT: Yale University Press.

Cross, R., Baker, W. and Parker, A. (2003) 'What creates energy in organizations?', *MIT Sloan Management Review*, **44**(4), pp. 51–56.

Flannery, R.B. (2012) *Posttraumatic Stress Disorder: The victim's guide to healing and recovery*, 2nd edn. New York: American Mental Health Foundation.

Fritz, C., Lam, C. and Spreitzer, G. (2011) 'It's the little things that matter: An examination of knowledge workers' energy management', *The Academy of Management Perspectives*, **24**(3), pp. 28–139.

Gailliot, M.T. and Baumeister, R.F. (2007) 'The physiology of willpower: Linking blood glucose to self-control', *Personality and Social Psychology Review*, **11**(4), pp. 303–327.

Hirschfeld, R.M.A., Williams, J.B.W., Spitzer, R.L., Calabrese, J.R., Flynn, L., Keck, P.E., Lewis, L., McElroy, S.L., Post, R.M., Rapport, D.J., Russell, J.M., Sachs, G.S. and Zajecka, J. (2000) 'Development and validation of a screening instrument for bipolar spectrum disorder: The Mood Disorder Questionnaire', *The American Journal of Psychiatry*, **157**(11), pp. 1873–1875.

Kinnunen, U., Feldt, T., de Bloom, J and Korpela, K. (2015) 'Patterns of daily energy management at work: Relations to employee well-being and job characteristics', *International Archives of Occupational and Environmental Health*, **88**(8), pp. 1077–1086. Available at: https://doi/org/10.1007/s00420-015-1039-9

Lanz, K. and Brown. P.T. (2020) *All the brains in the business: The engendered brain in the 21st Century organisation.* Switzerland: Palgrave Macmillan.

Loehr, J. and Schwartz, T. (2003) *The power of full engagement: Managing energy, not time, is the key to high performance and personal renewal.* New York: Free Press.

MacKinnon, D. (2018) *Depression in adults.* BMJ Best Practice. Available at: https://bestpractice.bmj.com/topics/en-gb/55

Maslach, C. and Leiter, M.P. (2016) 'Understanding the burnout experience: Recent research and its implications for psychiatry', *World Psychiatry*, **15**(2), pp. 103–111.

Maslach, C., Schaufeli, W.B. and Leiter, M.P. (2001) 'Job burnout', *Annual Review of Psychology*, **52**, pp. 397–422.

Mufson, L.H., Dorta, K.P., Moreau, D. and Weissman, M.M. (2011) *Interpersonal psychotherapy for depressed adolescents,* 2nd edn. New York: The Guilford Press.

Parker, A. and Gerbasi, A. (2016) 'The impact of energizing interactions on voluntary and involuntary turnover', *Management*, **19**(3), pp. 177–202.

Parker, S.L., Zacher, H., de Bloom, J., Verton, T.M. and Lentink, C.R. (2017) 'Daily use of energy management strategies and occupational well-being: The moderating role of job demands', *Frontiers in Psychology*, **8**, pp. 1–12. Available at: https://doi.org/ 10.3389/fpsyg.2017.01477

Quinn, R.W., Spreitzer, G.M. and Lam, C.F. (2012) 'Building a sustainable model of human energy in organizations: Exploring the critical role of resources', *The Academy of Management Annals*, **6**(1), pp. 337–396.

Riethof, N., Bob, P., Laker, M., Varakova, K., Jiraskova, T. and Rabock, J. (2019) 'Burnout syndrome, mental splitting and depression in female health care professionals', *Medical Science Monitor*, **25**, pp. 5237–5240. Available at: https://doi.org/10.12659/MSM.915360

Schaufeli, W.B. and Bakker, A.B. (2004) 'Job demands, job resources, and their relationship with burnout and engagement: A multi-sample study', *Journal of Organizational Behavior*, **25**(3), pp. 293–315.

Schippers, M.C. and Hogenes, R. (2011) 'Energy management of people in organizations: A review and research agenda', *Journal of Business and Psychology*, **26**(193), pp. 193–203. Available at: https://doi.org/10.1007/s10869-011-9217-6

Schulz, A.S., Bloom, J. and Kinnunen, U. (2017) 'Workaholism and daily energy management at work: Associations with self-reported health and emotional exhaustion', *Industrial Health*, **55**(3), pp. 252–264.

Selvaraj, S. (2021) *Bipolar disorder in adults.* BMJ Best Practice. Available at: https://bestpractice.bmj.com/topics/en-gb/488

Thayer, R.E. (1989) *The biopsychology of mood and arousal.* New York: Oxford University Press.

2
Influences on energy

THIS CHAPTER CONSIDERS THE MAIN INFLUENCES on energy that can impact executives in and out of the working environment (how these can be addressed in coaching is considered in the second half of the book). Helping clients understand their personal influences will further heighten their awareness of why they are feeling and behaving in a certain way and the impact that this has on their performance and can feed into the process of identifying courses of action. And the influences will be very personal: what will be exhausting for one person (like travelling for work) will be energising for another. All the quotes in this chapter are made by fellow executive coaches and reproduced with their permission.

The interrelated categories of influence

Four overall categories of influence have been identified, as illustrated in Figure 2.1, these being: physical; psychological both in terms of emotional and cognitive influence; occupational and those that occur outside of work. Although I have separated out influences into categories, they are often interrelated. For example, a client may be tired (physical) due to the stress caused by thinking about workload (cognitive) which potentially makes them angry or afraid (emotion), they may then manage this by frequently drinking alcohol (physical), which affects their sleep (physical) and this combination depletes their energy further. Another example being that our perception of our levels of physical energy can influence our energetic activation: when our physical energy reserves are depleted, and we realise this, it can be stressful, making one feel as if the pressures of life are too great and lead to anxiety, frustration and defensiveness.

> My clients don't get enough sleep. They overindulge in all sorts of substances. They work far too hard. They usually travel far too much. They're under extreme stress. And I don't think people understand that projects are different environments to normal business. In normal business you can always find an excuse for not meeting your targets. In a project you have a time, you have a dedicated time, you have a requirement you need to meet and it needs to bloody work, and you have a cost that is fixed. It is significantly more stressful. I've worked with

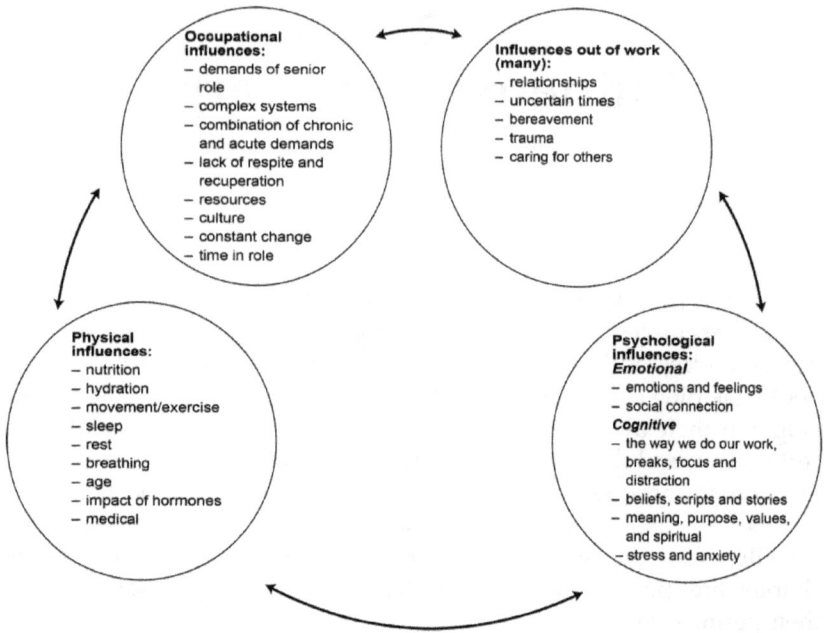

Figure 2.1 Influences on energy in the context of executive coaching

both and there is just no comparison. The very top of project management is vicious. You won't survive if you don't have enough energy. You just won't survive. And I've seen several go under.

Physical influences on energy

The main influences on physical energy identified in the literature are: nutrition; hydration; movement, including having enough exercise; getting enough sleep and rest; breathing; age; the impact of hormones and having a medical condition. These are summarised in Figure 2.2. Taking a restful break will be considered in Chapter 7.

These factors may occur in combination, there will be times when clients may not drink enough, eat well and have adequate sleep and this may impair performance and affect energy levels in a number of ways (Parry *et al.*, 2017; Parry *et al.*, 2018). Sometimes such impairment can have little or no impact but at other times this can be very serious leading to devastating consequences. For example, when there is a need to make difficult, split-second, important decisions when an error can have serious implications.

**Physical
influences:**
- nutrition
- hydration
- movement/exercise
- sleep
- rest
- breathing
- age
- impact of hormones
- medical

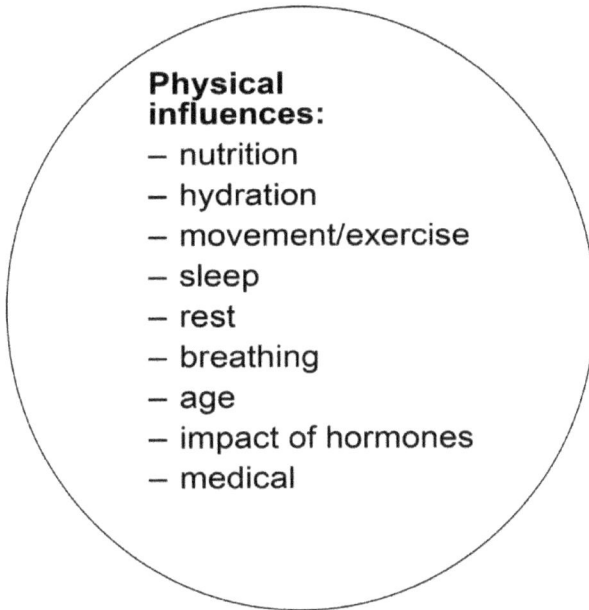

Figure 2.2 Physical influences on energy

Nutrition

Getting nutrition from our diet involves complex processes where food is broken down into constituent molecules and used for important bodily functions necessary for health and repair. One process being cellular respiration, when energy obtained from food is converted into energy used in the body's cells. For most of us, the more we eat a healthy, balanced, personalised diet the healthier we will be, with an obvious impact on the energy levels we experience. Where energy is concerned, diet has been shown to: impact performance (Parry *et al.*, 2017); self-control (Gailliot and Baumeister, 2007); heighten the risk of depression and impact emotional well-being (White, Horwath and Conner, 2013). In addition, a diet high in dietary trans fatty acids has been shown to increase the likelihood of irritability and aggression (Golomb *et al.*, 2012), states which can lead to inappropriate high energy.

And it's not just what we eat. Many busy clients skip lunch due to lack of time during the day, maybe following a rushed breakfast eaten on the go. Some may also be on diets. Missing meals slows the metabolic rate which leads to fewer calories being burned and the lowering of energy and motivation (Parry *et al.*, 2017).

Hydration

Water is a vital nutrient which accounts for over 60% of body mass and is important for the maintenance of physical energy, emotional and cognitive functioning (Parry et al., 2017). A deficit in water of just 2% of body weight has been shown to lead to sleepiness, impatience and apathy in research in dehydration accompanied by hyperthermia (Adolf, 1947). More recent studies have shown that mood states are affected when suffering even from mild dehydration (around 1% of body weight) which could be brought on by everyday activities. This has been shown to lead to heightened tension and anxiety, fatigue and inertia (Ganio et al., 2011) and have a negative effect on mood and cognitive performance (Adan, 2012; Benton and Young, 2015).

Despite drinking enough water being very important I suggest that often, in a busy work schedule, it is overlooked. Clients can forget to drink enough, maybe only remembering when they are thirsty and, as most of us know, when we are thirsty we may have been dehydrated for some time.

Movement and exercise

It is useful to think of movement-related physical health in two ways: how sedentary we are and how much we exercise.

Where being sedentary is concerned, most of our clients have sedentary working lives. Even if they run or go to the gym twice a week, they are sitting at their desks or in meetings for the best part of their day. This is exacerbated by working at home, with no journey to work, no office stairs to use when going to meetings and no need to walk any distance to get a coffee or lunch. It is interesting to consider, during the COVID-19 pandemic which started in 2020, how many people became more sedentary, sat in their home on calls for hours on end. This matters: prolonged sitting affects people's fitness levels regardless of whether they exercise or not and research indicates that two hours of sitting cancels out the benefits of 20 minutes of exercise for our cardiorespiratory fitness levels (Kulinski et al., 2014).

Even a little exercise boosts energy and research has shown that exercise decreases the onset of fatigue due to higher maximal oxygen intake and increases feelings of vigour (Lovelace, Manz and Alves, 2007). It also increases blood flow and therefore oxygen supply in the brain, positively impacts mood through physiological and biochemical mechanisms such as endorphin release and you think better when your movement is increased (Brandon and Loftin, 1991; Lovelace, Manz and Alves, 2007). It is worth noting that exercise is particularly beneficial, and more easily sustained (Parfitt and Gledhill, 2004), if it is enjoyed rather than thought to be a chore (Watkins, 2014), there's my excuse for avoiding aerobics classes then.

One of my clients was feeling very low in energy and mood. His preferred exercise was running but he told me that he wasn't enjoying this, it was actually making him feel worse. We laughed that he felt it was like running in flippers. He considered what he might do instead. Actually what he wanted to do was see his friends, but social contact had been lacking. He decided that, for now, going for walks with friends was the way forward.

Sleep

We all know that we need enough sleep to maintain health, perform well and feel energised, and this is backed up by many studies (Sonnentag, Binnewies and Mojza, 2008; Parry *et al.*, 2018). The exact amount of sleep someone might need is a personal matter and studies dispute what a 'normal' or 'right' amount of sleep should be, but most agree that anything less than five to seven hours is too short. As well as being a time when memories are consolidated (Sanches *et al.*, 2015), emotions moderated (Parry *et al.*, 2018) and learning is aided, sleep is a time of recovery and is when substantial growth and repair occurs, for example, at least one study (Fultz *et al.*, 2019) suggests that waste matter is removed in the deeper phases of sleep by the cerebral spinal fluid: waste matter which can be toxic for neurons.

Research suggests that a lack of sleep leads to poor functioning and I argue a knock-on effect on energy because it influences emotion, mood and cognition which are all linked to energetic activation. For example a lack of sleep:

- Can impact concentration levels, the ability to make decisions and other cognitive processing (Kuhnel *et al.*, 2017)
- Can have a negative impact on mental flexibility including the ability to adapt to change (Parry *et al.*, 2018)
- Affects motivation
- Leads to slower reaction times (Parry *et al.*, 2018)
- Is associated with disorders such as depression (Goldstein and Walker, 2014)

A lack of sleep is not necessarily just related to depleted energy. It may be an explanation for behaviours linked to inappropriate high energy. For example, a lack of sleep has been shown to:

- Affect the ability to moderate emotions and mood (Sanches *et al.*, 2015) including an increase in anger, impulsiveness and heightened irritability, even in low-stress situations (Goldstein and Walker, 2014)
- Be strongly related, when cumulative, to less effective leadership behaviour including a lack of moral reasoning and emotional intelligence and to destructive, passive-avoidant leadership behaviour (Olsen *et al.*, 2016)

- Lead to perceptions of invulnerability (Kadzielski, McCormick and Herndon, 2015)
- Heighten risk taking (Parry *et al.*, 2018)

Chronic sleep deprivation is worrying. And it is common, one study has found that a quarter of the population in France suffer from severe 'sleep debt' (Leger *et al.*, 2020). This is likely to build up as a result of a number of factors including: working very long hours with days that may include breakfast meetings and late nights in the office which also leave one wired and unable to get to sleep once in bed; having babies and small children to look after; medical causes; being menopausal or perimenopausal and getting older by the time one reaches sixty the average amount of sleep people have has decreased (Czeisler and Fryer, 2006). It has been suggested that the more we build up our sleep debt the less able we are to actually see that this is happening because we find it hard to remember what it is like to be fully rested and become unaware of the dangers. So we need to be able to both recognise, and make a conscious effort to 'repay', chronic sleep debt (Czeisler and Fryer 2006) although this can take a long time to do (Parry *et al.*, 2018).

However, as Czeisler stresses, organisations still expect their employees to function on low amounts of sleep. Many cultures encourage a working week of very long hours, seeing a need for rest and sleep as a weakness and confuse sleeplessness with vitality and high performance. Policies are not written and promoted that address organisational recommendations regarding sleep, including the length of hours worked, in spite of a lack of sleep being a proven danger to individual health and in some cases the health of others. For example, doctors and nurses have to work very long hours and executives walk into meetings after an overnight flight, in a different time zone, and are expected to perform immediately with no insistence for rest and recuperation after travelling, maybe having driven from the airport.

One of my clients had a remit which covered EMEA, European and American time zones. His emails never stopped and he was expected to attend meetings, and be on the top of his game, with colleagues all over the world at all times of the day and late in to the evening. No attention was paid to the impact that this might be having on his performance, energy and health: he was just expected to get on with it.

Breathing

It has long been known that breathing impacts our energy. Ancient traditions talk about life force and vital energy, sometimes called *prana* or *ch'i*, which were 'synonymous with respiration' (Nestor, 2020) and breathing techniques were taught to enhance energy alongside exercise and diet. Although little research has been conducted which looks at the quality of breathing from a medical perspective, and it is not mentioned in routine consultations with our general practitioners, there is now increased awareness that physical energy depends partly on the quality of our breathing. Breathing correctly helps balance the oxygen and carbon dioxide levels in the blood and is very important for energy levels and mental alertness. Watkins (2014), a cardiologist, states that one of the primary ways that we lose energy is through incoherent or erratic breathing and that if we want to improve this the quickest way to do so is to stabilise our breathing. Nestor (2020), author of *Breath: The New Science of a Lost Art* spent many years researching the science behind breath and the history of breathing. He found that many of us breathe incorrectly (for example, breathing through the mouth instead of the nose and shallow breathing) and that this can lead to depleted energy and cause or aggravate disease. Medical research supports this showing that shallow breathing does lead to fatigue and if the breathing is addressed by various respiratory exercises the fatigue can be reduced (Zakerimoghadam *et al.*, 2006): the more the exercises are done the more the fatigue intensity lessens.

It is interesting to note that it is suggested that shallow and erratic breathing, sometimes called 'email apnoea' due to the similarity to sleep apnoea (Nestor, 2020), can occur at work when the individual's attention is dispersed, maybe due to them checking their emails and social media. And the individual is usually not aware of this.

Age

There are a number of age-related factors which naturally affect our energy levels which are not related to clinical conditions. It could be that the client has 'seen it, done it' and doesn't really want to be doing that type of role anymore. Or, as one of my research partners pointed out, the resultant change in energy may not be problematic, just different. However, it is worth taking into account some age-related factors:

- As mentioned above, one implication of getting older is that we sleep less easily. Once we are over forty our sleep becomes more fragmented, we are more easily awakened and there is an increase in sleep disorders. And, for those who travel for work the circadian window for maintaining sleep narrows, meaning that we are more affected by travel across time zones and trying to sleep in a different circadian phase becomes more difficult (Czeisler and Fryer, 2006)
- Mitochondria generate 90% of the energy that the body and brain needs. These reduce in number as we age and the decline in numbers is also affected by environmental chemicals and toxins, poor diet, alcohol intake and smoking (Davenport, 2020)

I think the reality is for some people, if you turn the clock back twenty years, they wouldn't be saying the same things. They'd be coming at it with a different level of energy, focus and drive.

The quality of energy we might exhibit in our teens and twenties is very different to the quality of energy that we exhibit in later life. It doesn't mean that we are without energy. It just means that that quality of energy is being filtered in very, very many wonderful, different ways. So someone can be as energetic and more energetic in a different way in their eighties than in their twenties.

Impact of hormones: periods, menopause or perimenopause, pre- and postnatal depression

Women may be experiencing depleted or inappropriate high energy because of their periods, or symptoms of perimenopause or menopause. For example, where influences on energy are concerned, menstruation can result in symptoms such as depression, poor diet, sleep loss and chaotic behaviour. In over 20 years of coaching not one of my female clients has brought this up in a session. As a colleague mentioned to me, is it that they think that they "just have to get on with it"?

Prenatal depression and postnatal depression are also causes of depleted energy. Prenatal depression is not an unusual condition, one research paper found that 20% of women presenting in ten obstetric clinics showed signs of the condition (Marcus *et al.*, 2003).

I was very concerned about a coaching client who was about seven months pregnant. She was really lacklustre in a session and I started to be concerned. I told her what I was witnessing. She said that she was feeling really exhausted but it was more than tiredness, she was really out of sorts. She said that she had had a really bad experience with her first pregnancy and afterwards suffered from postnatal depression. She started to describe the 'symptoms' she was experiencing and to realise that these were very similar to those she had with postnatal depression. I suggested that she might need expert help. She self-referred for both an appointment with her General Practitioner and counselling with the company Employee Assistance Programme. She was diagnosed with prenatal depression. She could have carried on with the coaching but chose to have a break and we continued after her maternity leave.

Medical causes of depleted and inappropriate high energy

It is important for executive coaches to be aware of, but not pulled into diagnosing or hypothesising about, medical causes of depleted energy and inappropriate high energy (referred to as excessive energy from a medical perspective) and to encourage the client to see their doctor if necessary. The following section has been written for this book by two medical General Practitioners (the UK term for Primary Care Physicians) Dr Jane Jenkinson (MBChB) and Dr Daniel Jenkinson (MBChB) and is partly based on NICE guidelines (2020).

Depleted energy levels or a feeling of being 'tired all the time' is a common reason for consultation in General Practice. The most common causes are psychological, for example, stress, anxiety and depression but it is important to consider the physical causes. These can include almost any condition affecting organs such as the heart, lungs and digestive, rheumatological or neurological systems. It can also include endocrine conditions such as diabetes mellitus, hypothyroidism, disturbance of calcium metabolism and electrolyte abnormalities. Anaemia is frequently associated with depleted energy and further investigations are often required to determine the cause. Over the counter medication, particularly sedating antihistamines and codeine-containing pain relieving medication can be implicated alongside prescribed and illicit drugs. Excess alcohol and carbon monoxide poisoning should be considered. A history of tick bite and rash can raise the possibility of lyme disease. Red flags such as weight loss, fever, night sweats and lymphadenopathy raise the possibility of infection or malignancy and persistent fatigue with normal findings on examination and investigation points towards chronic fatigue syndrome.

Excessive energy is a much less frequent reason for consultation and in contrast to depleted energy levels has fewer causes to consider. Mania or hypomania should be suspected when excessive energy occurs in combination with elevated mood, irritability, rapid speech, intensity, lots of new ideas, uncharacteristic behaviour and excessive spending. Mania or hypomania is most commonly caused by bipolar disorder but can be drug induced as a result of steroids or stimulants such as caffeine and cocaine and can occasionally be a feature of multiple sclerosis. Anxiety can cause a person to feel 'driven' by high levels of nervous energy, often associated with other anxiety symptoms such as worry, dread, irritability, agitation, palpitations, tremor, sweating and insomnia. People with attention deficit hyperactivity disorder (ADHD) can also present with excessive energy, the hyperactive/impulsive aspect of the condition characterised by fidgeting, being unable to sit still, poor concentration and interrupting. The inattentive aspect is characterised by difficulty focusing and following instructions, mistakes, losing things and problems with organisation.

Finally, hyperthyroidism may present with excess energy, agitation, hyperactivity and sleep disturbance.

Patients presenting with depleted and excessive energy can expect a thorough history to be taken by their doctor and, where indicated, examination and blood tests or imaging to determine the cause.

Psychological influences

Where psychological influences on energetic activation are concerned, individuals will have their own complex psychological systems which consciously and subconsciously influence thought and behaviour. As illustrated in Figure 2.3, psychological influences are divided into two categories:

- emotional and
- cognitive/mental (the processing of information, the thinking)

As mentioned above, these are interrelated, for example, when one is angry (emotion) this may trigger thoughts (cognition) which together lead to behaviour and this may happen the other way round: what you think may generate emotions.

Psychological influences: emotional

Emotions are thought to be the main influence on energetic activation (Quinn, Spreitzer and Lam, 2012; Brown, Kingsley and Paterson, 2015). It is now widely accepted that emotions not only influence feelings and mood but are essential to human cognition (Bachkirova and Cox, 2007): influencing, or determining rationality, perception of events, thinking, decision-making and behaviour, mainly without us realising.

There is little agreement in the literature as to what is meant by 'emotion'. A useful working model identifying eight basic 'universal' or 'primary' emotions (in that they exist in some form from birth) has been produced in order to bring more clarity to the understanding of the emotions (Brown and Dzendrowskyj, 2018). The eight emotions are put into three categories. One being the 'attachment' or 'thrive' emotions – excitement/joy and love/trust – which allow people to perform and be closely involved with others in a positive way. Another, the five 'escape/ avoidance', or 'survival', emotions which are said to arise out of threat or deficit and are associated with safety, escape and avoidance, these being sadness, shame, disgust, anger and fear. And thirdly, surprise/startle, the 'potentiator' emotion, which is said to potentiate new thinking and behaviour, taking us either in the direction of escape/avoidance or attachment (Brown, Kingsley and Paterson, 2015). It is suggested that these primary emotions form the basis from which all feelings are derived, feelings being a complex compound of emotions, and also that all eight emotions can be experienced at the same time, for example, when someone is intensely jealous (Brown, Swart and Meyler, 2009).

Psychological influences:
Emotional
 – emotions and feelings
 – social connection
Cognitive
 – the way we do our work, breaks, focus and distraction
 – beliefs, scripts and stories
 – meaning, purpose, values, and spiritual
 – stress and anxiety

Figure 2.3 Psychological influences on energy

How emotions impact energy and performance

When we experience the attachment/thrive emotions, which I will from now on refer to as thrive emotions, we have the neurochemistry which is important for collaboration, engagement, nurturing, risk taking, performance and for being be 'in flow'. Flow is described as 'complete absorption in the present moment' (Nakamura and Csikszentmihalyi, 2009, p. 195). The accompanying neurochemistry being: oxytocin, a hormone that is involved in bonding and trust; dopamine, a neurotransmitter that results in excitement, joy and reward, helps sense-making and problem solving; and serotonin, which results in feelings of happiness (Rock, 2008; Lanz and Brown, 2020). These emotions are related to activation of the parasympathetic division of the Autonomic Nervous System (ANS) (Shiota *et al.*, 2011) which reduces a person's heart rate, enables rest and aids digestion.

Whereas in a 'survive state', the brain is not in its natural 'thrive state' and the focus is on protecting the individual (Brown, Swart and Meyler, 2009). In this state there is less oxygen and glucose available for brain functions which affects cognitive processing and the person is not fully accessing the prefrontal cortex thus hindering the higher functions necessary in leadership such as creativity (Brown and Lanz, 2019) and the ability to prioritise and problem solve. Other cognitive impacts include that it is more difficult to be in flow and the individual is less likely to be open to ideas and change. There is a negative impact on the ability to regulate emotion and people are more likely to be reactive than deliberate. Individuals are also less able to manage relationships effectively. In a survive state it is likely that there will be activation of the sympathetic division of the ANS or, as others refer to it, an autonomic state of defence. This results in flight and fight behaviours leading to defensive reactions (Rock, 2008) including hyper-arousal, showing as chronic anxiety, irritability and hypervigilance or freeze/submission reactions resulting in dissociation (also called disassociation), hypoarousal, numbness and withdrawal (Porges, 2020). In a survive state the body will produce the hormones cortisol and adrenalin, both of which can be energising (both appropriately and inappropriately) in the immediate and useful both for performance and keeping the individual safe with a multifaceted response to threat (Brown, Kingsley and Paterson, 2015). But if this continues over time, the chronic overproduction of both chemicals results in the inability to regulate them and they can become toxic. This may result in a significant drain of energy, depression, cognitive impairment and strain on biological systems (Michaud *et al.*, 2008).

Let's consider one of these survive emotions in more detail, anger (fear will be considered later in this chapter in the context of fear-based cultures). Anger can be energising, leading to appropriate high energy necessary for survival and coping with difficult situations including those in a work context. But it can also result in inappropriate high energy, for example, when someone is overly angry and in energy depletion. Where energy depletion is concerned, Childre and Rozman (2003) suggest that:

- Venting anger and coming down from an 'anger high' is draining
- Repressing anger takes energy to 'keep the fire' burning
- Projecting our worries into the future and then getting angry at what you expect will happen, 'emotional projection', using the same 'lens' to look forward as you had in the past, distorts perception of the current situation and this process drains a lot of energy
- One of the biggest energy drains and sources of anger at the 'self' is 'over-personalisation' which can lead to 'runaway emotions' for hours or days. This involves judging yourself 'as good or bad depending on how you reacted to a situation or how someone reacted to you' (Childre and Rozman, 2003, p. 73) and can lead to self-blame and shame. It can also block the ability to look at the bigger picture and reduce hopefulness

I had a client who used to get very angry at work. She mentioned to me that it used to take her up to two days to calm down, having been very angry, and that this was exhausting.

Clients may well have learnt to suppress emotion and feelings in childhood and throughout their careers. This takes effort (Hochschild, 1979; Grandey, 2000), can drain energy, may create confusion (Brown, Kingsley and Paterson, 2015) and has been linked to burnout (Hochschild, 1979).

In addition, displaying emotions that are not in line with how one really feels, emotional dissonance, can be exhausting. Despite their suppression these emotions and feelings will be just as influential for the individual (Brown, Kingsley and Paterson, 2015). Our clients may work in environments where deep suppression of emotion and feelings or the more superficial regulation of emotional expression is a requirement of their role. This is sometimes referred to as 'emotional labor', a term used to describe the management of emotions in response to rules within, or to meet the goals of, the organisation or because it is expected in their role (think how much doctors, nurses, therapists and judges have to suppress or regulate their emotions and their expression). The client may also work in an environment where being emotional is seen, incorrectly, to be the opposite of being rational (Grandey, 2000; Lanz and Brown, 2020) and where those who are more emotionally literate and expressive are perceived as being 'overly emotional' when actually, for some, their emotions might be just less buried.

The emotions are largely unconscious

A lot of the emotional influence on energetic activation will be unconscious. It was not until the nineteenth century that the concept of the unconscious was first described in both the fields of psychology and philosophy, prior to this all action was deemed to be conscious (Gardner, 2003). It is now proposed that in most cases 'action precedes reflection' by the conscious mind (Bargh and Morsella, 2008, p. 73) maybe up to ten seconds before the person becomes aware (Soon *et al.*, 2008). So very often we lack awareness of the emotions that underlie our responses. And these emotions are based on past learning and experience which can lead to emotion-driven responses which may not be wholly relevant to, nor be constructive for, the current context and this may influence our behaviour and the energy we experience at a given time.

Social influences on emotion

Human beings are deeply relational. Energy is influenced by positive relationships with others, leading to thrive emotions such as trust with the accompanying neurochemistry. Indeed research into influences on and strategies for 'energy management' in the workplace in the context of emotion have focused largely on the influence of relationships. High-quality relationships are described as ones with 'mutual positive regard, trust and active engagement' (Dutton, 2003). Such interactions do not have to be deep or intimate but could be just a single positive, meaningful interaction (Atwater and Carmeli, 2009). As well as leading to thrive emotions there are numerous other related benefits of supportive and positive social interactions which are related to energy. For example, they have positive impact on:

- Engagement
- Health both in the immediate and long term. Supportive interactions with others benefit immune, endocrine and cardiovascular functions (including reducing cardiovascular reactivity to stressors) and the encouragement of positive health behaviours (Umberson and Montez, 2010)
- Mental health including the lowering of stress (Umberson and Montez, 2010)
- The ability to have a sense of meaning and purpose (Umberson and Montez, 2010)
- Other colleagues involved in the interaction, with a self-generating loop where energy levels continue to increase for all parties (Cross, Baker and Parker, 2003; Dutton, 2003)
- Our ability to cope with threatening situations, enabling us to feel soothed due to the release of oxytocin (Gilbert, 2018). It is our biological imperative to connect and not be alone and this is particularly important in the case of reaction to threat. From an evolutionary perspective it means survival: there is safety in numbers

I had one client, he works incredibly hard, however he's got a wonderful family life and social life. It all works for him. But looking at it from the outside, we'd say he shouldn't be able to cope with the workload. But actually he's coped with it for years.

But there are many reasons why access to social connectedness might be difficult. Our client is likely to be in a senior position and this may mean that they do not feel able to truly connect with others due to their status; in addition their team may well be global with communication largely being virtual. Some of our clients may live alone or in some way feel socially isolated out of their working environment and this may be taking its toll, their social interaction may mainly be at work and with colleagues after work, so if this is affected in some way, such as during COVID-19 related lockdowns in 2020 and 2021, the toll of social isolation can be highly detrimental. Remote working, which is predicted to double post-pandemic (CIPD, 2020), obviously has an effect on social interaction and may lead to a loss of social connection. There will be a number of factors at play. For example, we are able to pick up less emotional and physical sensory data and cues from others on a 2D screen (particularly when talking to more than one person) which will also make it more difficult to assess the impact we are having on others. Also we may have less data about what people are thinking and doing because we aren't seeing colleagues in open plan offices and there will be less opportunity to have informal conversations. Having less data from the interaction often means that we fill the information gaps to make some sense of what is going on in the relationship and create a narrative which relies on prior experience and imagination, making it much more likely that we make assumptions. People may also fear that they are being excluded, particularly if their other colleagues are together, and be anxious that some colleagues are having more contact with senior people in the organisation.

She lives on her own. Her only contact in person during lockdown has been a weekly session with her personal trainer in the park. She's feeling really flat and is desperate to get back into the office.

Depleted energy, I think is because of lack of supportive relationships. This reminds me of one client who was on his knees metaphorically, he was feeling really isolated, fearful and anxious that he would end up missing something and make a mistake. His was the sort of job where a mistake might have cost his company millions. He was on high alert, feeling threatened and unable to talk to colleagues about what was really going on for him. He had very little social interaction with anyone at work and actually no time to see his friends out of work. His boss, a really abrasive, tricky guy, would often ignore him in the office, providing no connection and his sense of threat already experienced was exacerbated – imagine what a smile and a hello might have done instead.

Our clients may be in poor relationships with others both in and out of work and this can have a negative effect on energy. Research suggests that corrosive relationships at work, where there is no trust and a disregard of the other's worth (Dutton, 2003), seriously impact energy and well-being and 'are like black holes that deplete psychological resources' (Fritz, Lam and Spreitzer, 2011. p. 35). Poor relationships have been shown to be very stressful, impact physical health and lead to engagement in unhealthy behaviours as a coping strategy (Umberson and Montez, 2010). This may then have a knock-on effect on the individual's ability to work and on their other relationships. Being around political behaviour is suggested to be particularly draining

(Cross, Baker and Parker, 2003) as is being with others suffering from burnout (Maslach *et al.*, 2001).

Even positive social interactions at work may have negative consequences: a client who is seen as the 'go to person' could result in them being asked to take on more and more and being in the role of helper or rescuer which can result in overload and exhaustion. And lastly, social interactions may encourage poor health-related behaviour such as increased alcohol consumption when socialising after work.

Psychological influences: cognitive

Our conscious and unconscious cognitive processes have a significant impact on energetic activation, depleting energy and also leading to heightened, sometimes inappropriately high, energy levels. It is generally accepted that 'cognitive' refers to the active processing of information from the environment which is influenced by knowledge, experience, emotion and neurochemistry and results in perceptions, memories, thoughts and behaviours (with resultant neurochemistry). As with emotions, many influences on cognition will be unconscious, influenced by unconscious behavioural impulses and complex judgements made outside of awareness (Bargh and Morsella, 2008). These neural networks are reinforced through repeated use, resulting in habitual, unconscious patterns of thinking (Swart, Chisholm and Brown, 2015).

Research into cognitive influences on energy has in the past focused on work-related interventions such as having a break and ways of managing work, as previously mentioned. Breaks and how we organise our work can influence us mentally, this is relevant, but surely cognitive influences on energy are also more complex, we need to consider what influences the way we think. However, these more simple influences cannot be overlooked so this is where I will start.

The way we do our work

The way clients work can influence their energy. Some of this will be obvious and often tackled in executive coaching, such as the importance of effective prioritisation of tasks (more of this in Chapter 7), having a tendency for micro-management and whether the client is able to delegate appropriately and effectively.

NOT TAKING BREAKS

How many of us coach clients who do not take breaks during the working day, rush from one meeting to the next and eat lunch at their desks (and also in coaching sessions)? I am guessing that for most coaches this is what we experience as the norm. But breaks are important. They have been shown to have many benefits including the stopping of further energy depletion, aiding recovery and lessening the stress and fatigue that result from continual demands being made on people (Kim, Park and Niu, 2017). Not only is this relevant to people in the physical workplace but also to those working at home whose days are full of virtual meetings with no breaks in between. Recent research looking at brainwave activity conducted by Microsoft Human Factors Lab (2021) has confirmed that stress increases and accumulates during a session of back-to-back virtual meetings leading to fatigue, but that breaks helped to prevent this (more of this in Chapters 6 and 7). Whereas starting a meeting without a break in between led to high stress due to the knowledge that straight away you have to start another meeting, change topic and focus on something new.

BEING INTERRUPTED AND NOT FOCUSING

Not being able to both focus and manage interruptions when working can be draining (Schippers and Hogenes, 2011) and raise cortisol and adrenalin levels (Kline, 2020) which, as we have seen, can be detrimental over time. In addition, both can prevent one getting into flow, being engaged and reduce efficiency. Our clients may be constantly disturbed, not only by colleagues in person, but by emails and phone-related activity in an age of constant connectivity. It is likely that many of us spend at least a couple of hours per day responding to emails and checking social media, the psychological reward in this case being interaction or information. Even when we try to limit how much we look at our emails it can still be stressful because the behaviour is so ingrained into our day: one study suggested that people experienced less stress if they checked their emails fewer times a day but they continued to experience what the researchers called 'telepressure' (Kushlev and Dunn, 2015), feeling the need to respond immediately. Telepressure was associated with a decrease in sleep quality, more sick days and the likelihood of mental and physical burnout.

As well as being disturbed there will be other reasons why our clients find it difficult to focus, one being the need to constantly scan the environment in order to not to miss anything. Such 'continuous partial attention' (Stone, 2007) has even been shown to affect breathing as mentioned above. Difficulty focusing can present problems particularly for people who are 'segmentors', who perform better when they have a clear boundaries around work activities and distinction between work and non-work, rather than 'integrators' who are more likely to flourish when juggling different activities (Rothbard, Phillips and Dumas, 2005).

More complex mental influences

THE STORIES WE TELL

The stories we tell ourselves (and others), our scripts, beliefs and set patterns of thought are hugely influential to how we live our lives, influencing us emotionally and cognitively, with the knock on effect on energetic activation. These stories will have been created over many years, some in childhood by authority figures such as parents and teachers or by people within our friendship groups and most likely become part of our narrative without us recognising that this is influencing who we see ourselves to be. Many of the stories that are influential will be based on assumptions, many of which will be 'untrue assumptions we live as true' (Kline, 2020, p. 78). Kline suggests that if we don't identify and question an assumption 'it will mature into the full creature: a belief', the latter being a view that is very difficult to question and is restrictive to fresh and independent thinking.

These beliefs may translate into self-criticism and a lack of self-compassion which can have a detrimental impact on energy due to the thinking process, along with the underlying survive emotions, stimulating the threat response. Self-criticism can also lead to 'drive' behaviours such as striving and perfectionism which may leave the individual little time for rest, recuperation or thinking. This may be behind the behaviour of some of our clients who are pushing themselves really hard, and driving those around them with little empathy and awareness. It is interesting to note that a lack of self-compassion can be more likely in stressful contexts such as when one is overloaded with work and not having enough recovery time and also in those who have a heightened or sensitised response to threat due to past life events including trauma and lack of affection (Gilbert, 2018).

MEANING AND PURPOSE IN ONE'S WORK

Finding life to be meaningful has been suggested to be both a cognitive and emotional assessment of whether one's life has purpose (a component of meaning) and value, and is consistently rewarding in some way (Baumeister *et al.*, 2013): this being judged against a backdrop of the individual's values and the cultural expectations of the society they live in. Research (and experience) suggests that life being experienced as meaningful could be as a result of numerous factors such as contributing to the welfare of others, being involved in culturally valued activities (Baumeister *et al.*, 2013) and from doing things that express and reflect one's identity.

Where work is concerned, having meaning and purpose, feeling like work matters and makes a difference to others, has been found to influence employee energy (Fritz, Lam and Spreitzer, 2011), engagement and intrinsic motivation (Cartwright and Holmes, 2006). For some, a real belief in their cause is highly energising. A lack of meaning may be due to the client not having connection to their employing organisation's philosophy and way of doing things; it may lack personal relevance and importance. It could also be that the client used to find their work meaningful but doesn't now that they are in a more senior role, no longer doing what they most enjoyed and felt passionate about, for example, a client in a senior teaching role and no longer having time with the students in the classroom. One of my clients spoke about losing the 'buzz' and energy they got from work having had to "hang up my boots and no longer be on the pitch" because they were now managing those making the deals rather than doing this personally.

> *Fifty-year-olds who have made it to the top, this has been their life mission. They have become CEOs and they think, "Well, what's that all about"? Some of them need to look for something entirely different. Some of them jump ship. I had one client who became a vicar.*

It has been suggested that the most compelling source of meaning and purpose is spiritual, 'the energy derived from connecting to deeply held values and a purpose beyond one's self-interest' (Loehr and Schwartz, 2003). Existential meaning, achieved through inner fulfilment from devotion to something perceived as being of value, is energising and research suggests that it gives a person the persistence and ability to continue with their work even when they are feeling fatigued or exhausted (Riethof *et al.*, 2019). For some, such deeper meaning is now sought at work rather than being provided by religion. But for many this is hard to find, leaving an 'existential vacuum', a deficit of meaning in both work and life. It is worth noting that having such a deficit of meaning is, for some, connected to the development of late-stage burnout (Langle, 2003; Riethof *et al.*, 2019).

Meaning, purpose and decision-making are underpinned by our values, 'complex cognitive and emotional constructs shaped by our experiences and the societies and cultures which form our environment' (Swart, Chisholm and Brown, 2015), which are often subconscious. Being driven by our values at work can result in engagement, easier decision-making and energetic activation.

Although having meaning and purpose in one's work is thought to be energising, this is not always the case. Baumeister *et al.* (2013) found that unlike happiness, living a meaningful life, but one which involves activities which are perceived to be unpleasant, can increase an individual's stress and anxiety and reduce happiness even when working towards a highly desirable goal such as helping others in need. It has also been suggested that experiencing too much meaning, and as a consequence not being able to decide between various priorities, can lead to exhaustion (Riethof et al., 2019). So although being unable to identify meaning and purpose in one's work can lead to low energetic activation and poor motivation it doesn't mean that having a meaningful working life is the panacea for energy. Maybe, if thought relevant to a particular client's energy, encouraging them to consider small aspects of meaning and purpose is all that they need (more on this in Chapter 7).

STRESS AND ANXIETY

We all encounter stress in our daily lives, in and out of work: it is natural and unavoidable and has many sources both from the past and in the current moment (some of which may activate past stress reactions which we may or may not be conscious of). The related state of anxiety is a physiological stress response which is a normal reaction to threat (Arroll and Kendrick, 2018) and is not deemed to be problematic unless the reaction is out of proportion to the level of threat, such as with phobias and Post-Traumatic Stress Disorder (PTSD), or the symptoms are causing disruption to the person's life and functioning, such as causing frequent panic attacks. In this case assessment, and in some instances treatment, will be required.

Stress and anxiety can impact energy in a number of ways resulting in optimal, appropriate energy if there is a positive and constructive response to the stressor which can enable performance ('eustress') or lead to inappropriate high energy or depleted energy if there is a negative response ('distress'). Executive coaches hear about many types of stressor that their clients experience, such as concern that they are doing the right thing, the impact of long working hours, deadlines, relationships and workload: these will be further considered in the next section of this chapter.

The impact of a stressor has a lot to do with how an individual appraises the stressor, reacts to it and copes with it both emotionally and cognitively, with (di)stress resulting from a perception that the environment is taxing or exceeding one's resources and endangering well-being (Lazarus and Folkman, 1984; Kupriyanov and Zhdanov, 2014). It is useful to consider stress as a dynamic process which reflects the internal process of the individual, external factors including the intensity and duration of the stressor, and how these interact. Some reactions can create a vicious circle which maintains, and maybe exacerbates, problematic levels of stress (Butler, 1993). For example, when a person is self-critical or ruminates about their stress, thinking, amongst other things, that they should be able to cope, it can raise the level of (di)stress and increase the likelihood of consequent survive emotions (Du *et al.*, 2018). Also, if the client's response includes problematic coping strategies such as working longer hours, this can lead to the individual becoming more tired and working more slowly or becoming irritated with colleagues and damaging relationships with those around them. Additional influencing factors include whether the stressor is uncontrollable, intense, short-lived or chronic, cumulative (the more 'life events' experienced over the past 3 years, the more vulnerable a person may be to distress, Butler, 1993) and the accompanying emotions. Care needs to be taken to recognise when a client's capacity to cope with increasing demands becomes over-stretched, their ability to function deteriorates (Butler, 1993) and collapse or exhaustion is likely. In this case referral may well be necessary.

When negative, the impact of stress can be physiological; cognitive (for example, impaired concentration, hypervigilance, lacking enthusiasm); emotional with accompanying low mood (for example, being angry or afraid) and behavioural (including being agitated, irritable, socially withdrawn and having speech problems). If clients experience (dis)stress their energy levels are very often depleted and their capacity to concentrate is less.

> *(I worked with) a guy who had been given a big new job, expected to take on an awful lot more, but not being paid for it, or recognised for it. And his energy was severely impacted. Physically, he wasn't sleeping very well. So he was tired. And he recognised that he was tired. And he just felt very, very stressed and under threat the whole time.*

The occupational context – what might be happening to and around people

Influences on physical energy and energetic activation obviously happen within a context. Contextual influences will be both work-related and outside of work, in the individual's personal life. Let us start with the occupational context (Figure 2.4).

The general demands of a senior role

Executives face many challenges which they may bring to coaching: they work within complex systems; balance conflicting pressures from stakeholders (Stokes and Jolly, 2014); manage multiple relationships and are under pressure to perform. In Chapter 3 there is a long list of the expectations and responsibilities of senior executives and this highlights that the role of senior executives is highly complex, the demands being even greater during times of recession, economic crisis and/or global pandemic: factors which may also mean that their positions are under threat. In addition, these external demands may be accompanied by their own internal pressures such as a drive to succeed maybe for status and fear about survival in the organisation. This could result from an expectation that people at their level in organisations are not expected to be in post for that long (research by Xueming, Kanuri and Andrews, 2013, suggested that CEOs generally need to move on after an average of 5 years).

Occupational influences:
- demands of senior role
- complex systems
- combination of chronic and acute demands
- lack of respite and recuperation
- resources
- culture
- constant change
- time in role

Figure 2.4 Occupational influences on energy

Research supports the experience of many coaches and executives that working in these demanding roles is very energy intensive and the job demands can lead to negative impacts, both energy depletion (Lee, Ashforth and Blake, 1996; Sonnentag, Binnewies and Mojza, 2010) and inappropriate high energy due to increased energy arousal (manifesting in increased heart rate and adrenalin excretion) which sometimes cannot be appropriately channelled due to constraints in the work environment (Lovelace, Manz and Alves, 2007). There are many factors which contribute to the demands on energy for those in senior roles, including:

- The need to work long hours which also reduces opportunity for recovery (Fritz, Lam and Spreitzer, 2011)
- Operating in complex environments: a longitudinal study by Li, Burch, and Lee (2017) has shown that increased complexity in roles is associated with job strain and energy depletion
- The increased use of technology means that emails and social media feeds follow you around in your pocket (Fritz, Lam and Spreitzer, 2011)

- The need to embrace rapid technological change (de Bloom, Kinnunen and Korpela, 2015)
- The use of higher-order executive brain functions that are very energy intensive such as self-regulation, active initiative and effortful choosing (Brown, Kingsley and Paterson, 2015; Gailliot and Baumeister, 2007). Making many decisions (which may have far reaching implications) in particular has been shown to leave the person in a depleted state (Vohs *et al.*, 2014)
- The exercising of self-control, altering one's responses deliberately to bring them in to line with set standards, for example, when resisting impulses, controlling emotions, coping with stress, dealing with others and being continuously vigilant. This has been shown to require a constant exertion of energy and also to lower blood glucose levels with a subsequent impact on neurotransmission and the lowering of necessary resources for brain activity (Boyatzis, Smith and Blaize, 2006; Baumeister, Vohs and Tice, 2007)
- Time pressure and work overload which can lead to a state of threat because the individual thinks that they will not meet their goals or targets, with a potential knock-on effect of self-criticism (Lee, Ashforth and Blake, 1996; Sonnentag, Binnewies and Mojza, 2010)
- 'Power stress' caused by two factors: firstly, the need to regularly exercise self-control, as mentioned above, and secondly, compassion fatigue, when addressing the emotional needs of others leads to feeling overwhelmed (McClelland, 1985)
- Excessive demands combined with a lack of control (both perceived and actual). For example, many will lack control over approaching deadlines or organisational policies and their implementation, such as overseeing the lay-off of staff when they do not think that this is the right thing to do. This has been shown to have an accompanying impact on physical health, in particular cardiovascular disease, and psychological health (Lovelace, Manz and Alves, 2007)

The combination of chronic and acute demands

Such chronic demands are a prominent cause of energy depletion in senior executives, with clients feeling like they have to be constantly on tap, needing to have answers and be able to respond twenty-four hours a day. In addition, my research suggests that senior clients have to cope with both chronic and acute demands, urgent matters that immediately need attending to, and this combination has a significant impact on client energy levels. This may be accompanied by the thinking that one just has to keep going in order to meet deadlines, get through the day's meetings and get through the in-tray, despite feeling tired.

There is the relentlessness that is like the underlying drumbeat. And then there's these big things that come, like a deadline today, or go here, go there.

Where the combination of chronic and acute demands is concerned, people can have very high appropriate energy levels when responding to a crisis, such as health service employees initially responding to the COVID-19 pandemic, but this is not sustainable for a long time and can result in high fatigue levels. In crisis situations there is also a tendency to over-give, but the more we do this the more likely it is that we get overtired or conversely, completely 'wired'. In such situations there is a real need for the conscious consideration of personal energy levels and how these can be addressed.

Lack of respite and recuperation

But do people take energy renewal seriously? I assume that most understand that it is very important to rest and recuperate and that not doing so can result in depleted energy, as supported by research (de Bloom, Kinnunen and Korpela, 2015). But it is my experience that this is often overlooked by those who work: most athletes build in recuperation, they avoid overtraining, but those in senior positions generally don't. There are numerous reasons why this might be, including:

- Senior executives believe that within their organisation it is not okay to take time out nor to look after oneself
- The incessant pace of work, and of change, results in clients not being able to shut off from work for enough time to be able to recover or do activities that are energising
- The need for downtime is no longer being acknowledged by society
- Job insecurity may make it less likely that people take time off for recovery
- Having to care for others such as children or elderly relatives when they get home means that there is little time for recuperation or energising activities
- People find it very difficult to switch off. This is in part influenced by more people now working from home and lacking the 'stop cues' like reading the paper on the train home from work, the walk from the station to the house or listening to the radio in the car

The emotional impact that it takes when you've delivered and you've expended a lot of energy. And then you go into this darker place where your energy reserves are low and you have to recharge your batteries.

Now that's all gone. I'm not saying that the human impact has gone. What's gone is the recuperation time. And even the concept that you need to.

What you observe in organisations is that 'we've' now got to focus on our objectives for next year regardless of whether it's been a good year or a bad year. So there just never seems to be a place where a bit of respite is okay. We seem to have short-circuited all of those things which perhaps were built into an older map or model of the way people do business. But having downtime just seems to be bleeding its way out of our language.

Resources

The perception of how well resourced one is to be able to achieve one's goals can influence energy (Quinn, Spreitzer and Lam, 2012). Resources not only being financial and human but also those which both reduce job demands and stimulate personal learning and development (Kinnunen *et al.*, 2015). For example, if a client thinks that they are under-resourced, their budget is insufficient, they do not have enough team members or have not been given enough authority, this may result in them getting very tired or conversely running around like a 'headless chicken' trying to do everything. A perception of a chronic imbalance between demands and resources has been shown to lead to disabling (di)stress which makes it more likely that a (di) stress reaction is experienced when other work-related demands come the person's way, with a risk of fatigue, demoralisation and cognitive effects (Butler, 1993).

Culture

The culture or system in which the client works, which could be the organisational culture or the culture within their team or management team, can have a significant cognitive and emotional impact on energetic activation and may be significantly related to the individual being able to find the work meaningful, purposeful and aligned to their values. I will consider some examples below and I am sure that most executive coaches could come up with many case studies where organisational culture has impacted client energy. Clients may be optimally energised, perceiving the organisation culture as positive or speak of unethical behaviour, poor communication, management incompetence, little appreciation of the need for work-life balance, those in senior levels not doing what they say they are going to do and role conflict. This may be accompanied by a cultural expectation that the employee's natural emotional and behavioural responses should be suppressed and that they should just get on with it.

Top-down approach

It is suggested that workplace cultures that impose direction and drive people from above, assuming that people are agents of, and should be directing their energy towards, the organisation's goals do not engage human energy. Those working in such cultures who think that they are not involved and feel that they lack autonomy can, as a result, be less energised than those who believe that they are actively involved (Lanz and Brown, 2020).

Interpersonal dynamics

Working in a culture where the behaviour of others is damaging (for example, bullying or very critical), where there are difficult interpersonal dynamics, conflicting roles and where one doesn't feel valued by others can lead to people feeling under threat and affect energetic activation. In these situations it is much more likely that employees will be in survive rather than thrive state. For example, working in trust-scarce environments can lead to energy depletion or the raising of energy with people being very wary and agitated, constantly scanning for danger. And when positive interaction with others is lacking, this is one powerful method of raising energetic activation which is absent.

> I was working with a very senior guy in a manufacturing company. There was weariness in the organisation I think, a herd working pattern that many people fell into. It was the kind of place that bruised you as a culture. And this guy, you could see the age written on his face. It was hard and it was tiring and therefore what I never picked up was massive amounts of enthusiasm about anything.

> In the second session I asked the client what impact the culture was having on him. I suspected that the culture was toxic. He was pale, withdrawn and very serious. He started to describe the organisation and after a bit of time he started to cry. He was used to being in control, being seen as incredibly clever and successful academically but in this organisation, which he had recently joined, he didn't know where he stood with people. He was constantly being criticised for behaviours such being serious (he was actually very funny), being focused purely on the argument that he was trying to make and being over-cautious: behaviours that only got more common the more the 'flack' came his way. He was rapidly losing all confidence and was very tired and upset.

Fear-based cultures

Experiences at work all too commonly trigger a fear response. Many work in cultures where there is a fear of failure, of making mistakes, that comes from the very top. In these cultures employees are driven by fear. We as coaches might know that this is unsustainable but this doesn't mean that we always see true will for organisational change. As considered earlier in this chapter, experiencing threat and being fearful leads people to be in a survive state and this is not conducive to having optimal energy particularly when the experiencing is chronic.

The human brain is constantly scanning for danger, a process led by a specific part of the brain, the central and medial amygdala (Michaud *et al.*, 2008) and this is usually based on past experience: 'embedded in the amygdala are all the fear-based events we've ever experienced; stored as neuronal patterns available to be triggered at any time throughout life' (Brown, Kingsley and Paterson, 2015, p. 19). When threat is detected and fear results, the person's blood pressure increases, the process of cortisol and adrenalin production is instigated, the ANS is activated and the movement centres of the body engaged to allow an appropriate physical response to danger in the form of energy and strength to allow flight or fight (Brown, Kingsley and Paterson, 2015). At the same time danger signals are processed by the medial and orbital prefrontal cortex, which allows appraisal of the stressor and sense-making through thought and the formation of both learning and memory associated with fear and anxiety (Nader *et al.*, 2000). These processes, working in conjunction, allow both survival responses and decision-making to occur. This is useful in the immediate but detrimental when chronic.

My client was on the board of their organisation. You never knew when you were going to be verbally attacked in meetings by the CEO. It could just come out of the blue. All of them sat in meetings on tenterhooks, fearful that it might be their turn. It was exhausting. And these were very senior people.

When I started coaching one particular client their organisation had just conducted a 360 process for senior management which was organised by an outside agency. She was feeling so vulnerable anyway but on top of this she knew that her 360 report was going to be read by her boss and the members of the board before her. I couldn't believe that the process had been organised in this way. She was fearful about what they were going to be talking about behind her back. There was no trust whatsoever and the impact on her was massive.

Discriminatory cultures

Working in cultures where you are excluded, discriminated against or in which you have to conform and do not think that you can be yourself may affect clients in a number of ways. This may include inappropriate high energy due to anger ('I'll prove them wrong'), or fatigue ('I'm not sure I can do this anymore'). Not thinking that you can be yourself and feeling the need to create a façade of conformity can cause psychological distress that can be draining (Hewlin, 2003). In some cases, our clients may be trying to behave in a way that is not playing to their strengths. For example, Lanz and Brown (2020), in their book *All the Brains in the Business* make a powerful argument for organisations needing to enable women to bring their strengths to their organisation, instead of wasting their corporate energies being the best men they can be, why not turn those energies into being the real women they can be and see how they could arrive at the same places as men – if that's where they want to get to – but doing it their way. (Lanz and Brown, 2020 p. 36)

Cultures that push you and push you

Working in performance-driven cultures where this is all that seems to matter, and the work is continually piled on, has been likened to running the risk of being like a car that is driven in top gear under all conditions up a hill 'when the hill gets too steep, the foot goes harder on the accelerator' (Lanz and Brown, 2020, p. 117). But those of us who have been in cars straining up a hill know that at some point the engine starts to let off a lot of steam or smoke and the car can grind to a halt (or go backwards, rolling back down the hill in the Lake District, but that's another story). This is not sustainable.

> *We are tied into this narrative of 'it's better to be faster than smarter'. It's not okay to take time out. It's not okay to look after ourselves. We've got to look after everybody else except ourselves.*

> *My client worked in a high-pressure organisation, things were never good enough, the head of the organisation was often screaming at someone, often in front of others, the work piled on and you never knew when you were going to get it in the neck. The impact this had on the client was that they became 'wired', agitated and were constantly waiting for the next blow, both at work and at home. They were not easy to be around. This had to be brought to their attention but it wasn't easy to do so.*

Constant change

Significant and continual change, for example, due to organisational mergers, reorganisation and restructuring can impact employee energy. This may be because of the resultant workload and intense emotion due to a number of factors such as job insecurity, guilt (Bridges, 2009) and cynicism (Cartwright and Holmes, 2006). It is also useful to note that it has been suggested that employees are unable to start new projects with full energy and attention until the previous ending is completed.

The organisation had been through a massive downsizing exercise right across the world. And they were then entering into another level of change almost immediately after that.

I think one of the things that makes people tired is when the organisation goes round the same merry-go-round it's been round multiple times. And they never seem to get to the place they want to be and yet here we are again in the same vortex and the same cycle.

Length of time in post

The length of time someone has been in their position within their organisation may be an influence, some may be jaded because they have been in the organisation too long and others may find that having a new role affects their energy.

I worked with a guy who was in a new role and not coping. He talked to me a lot about what he had done to look after himself. But he was worried he was going to have a heart attack or something similar. And he realised that he needed to do something about this.

I don't know if this is just an age thing or if it is about being jaundiced about being in an organisation too long. Both I think are major factors in how people present around this stuff. But I think what you see is a decline in ambition.

The context – influences out of work

There are so many influences on energy levels that could be happening outside of the working environment such as: chronic or acute ill health; relationship difficulties; bereavement; experiencing trauma and so on. I cannot cover all in this book but have focused on some that may occur (see the summary in Figure 2.5).

Living in uncertain times

I am sitting in my office writing when there is global upheaval: the COVID-19 pandemic is having a massive global impact; the climate crisis is worsening and there are political crises around the world. I am witnessing great hardship unfolding globally. And each and every one of us is impacted in some way. Yet this state of global upheaval is currently the context in which our clients are still expected to perform, make excellent decisions, inspire and lead.

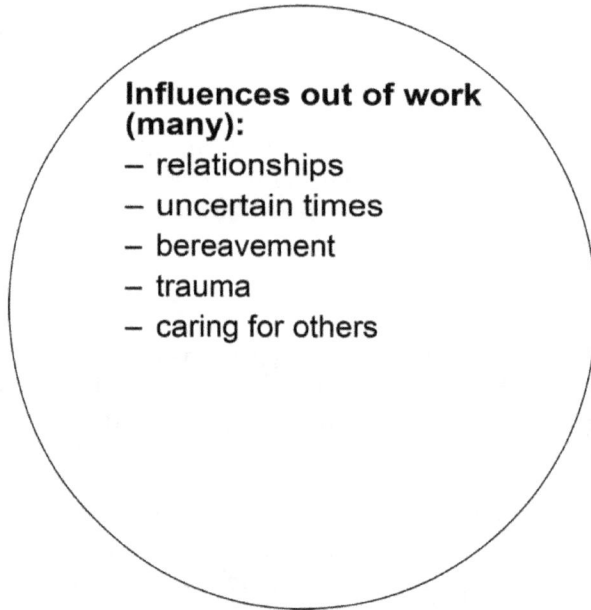

Figure 2.5 Influences on energy out of work

Take the COVID-19 pandemic. Porges (2020) described the pandemic as being 'devastating' for our nervous system eliciting threat responses, interfering with our ability to be optimistic and affecting the ability to co-regulate and feel safe with others. It challenged us socially, emotionally and cognitively, admittedly some much more than others. For most of us there was more ambiguity when actually humans generally much prefer certainty, we didn't know what was coming next and planning was nigh on impossible: one of my clients was given three hours to close their numerous UK stores just before Christmas 2020 at the height of the shopping season and at the same time had to make sure that all orders could be fulfilled online. Another had been involved in deciding how all their UK employees were going to work remotely, then not remotely but safely, then remotely again over a matter of a few weeks. We naturally look for ways to fix situations we find ourselves in and in this context it was hard to find solutions. Anecdotally I heard people describe themselves as feeling energised, galvanised, at the start of the first UK lockdown in March/April 2020 (I guess the flood of adrenalin and cortisol helped) and then the drop in energy came, the 'what next' just got too much, the lack of social contact with colleagues and hugs from friends and family took its toll as did the worry, the uncertainty and the not knowing. We could not follow some of our current habits and the formation of new habits is harder. We were on high alert for danger but it was a danger caused by something we could neither see nor control.

Situations which bring instability and require us to do things differently result in hypervigilance and heightened emotions and this takes more energy. Again, in the case of the COVID-19 pandemic some of our clients may have coped well, for example, enjoying working from home and not having to commute. Some may have experienced great distress. For others they may have experienced a sense of 'languishing' as described in Chapter 1 (Keyes, 2002; Grant, 2021). Languishing is a concept which has been re-used to describe how some people felt as a result of the pandemic, including living in lockdown, a situation that became no longer acute but chronic. It is described as an absence of well-being and thriving (Grant, 2021), just going through the motions without feeling good about it, with no meaning, purpose or aim and a sense of emptiness, lack of motivation, focus, dulled emotion and a feeling of stagnation. This is in contrast to 'flourishing' (when you are in relationship with others and have a strong sense of both meaning and mastery) and also to depression.

As already explored in this chapter, people need social connection. One of the reasons why the pandemic was so hard to cope with for many (not all), explained from a polyvagal perspective, is that it presented a paradoxical challenge to the nervous system (Porges, 2020). The human biological imperative is to connect with others when faced with threat. In order to co-regulate our neurophysiological state, positive two-way social interaction, particularly via vocal intonation and facial expression is needed to move from a state of danger to feeling safe and calm. The paradox is that this very connection creates another threat, that of infection, which means we can't fulfil the biological drive. Without such social connection, without the co-regulation downgrading innate reactions to threat, people may become defensive and exhibit flight or fight responses which could also be reflected in chronic anxiety and irritability. If these fight or flight reactions do not result in the individual feeling safe this can escalate the individual's reaction into an immobilised state which can include 'withdrawal, loss of purpose, social isolation, despair, and depression' (Porges, 2020, p. 136).

An additional cognitive impact of the COVID-19 pandemic has been described which is sometimes referred to as 'brain fog' (Sarner, 2021). Again, this is a normal reaction to a collective traumatic experience and the contraction of most aspects of life. Brain fog is characterised by poor memory, attention and problem solving accompanied by overall dullness and lifelessness. It is thought to be the result of a number of factors resulting from the pandemic, including: the lack of stimulation usually gleaned from new experiences and distinctiveness within the day meant that we stopped paying attention; most had reduced social interaction and thirdly, the brain probably had to work harder if in virtual meetings and online social interactions due to poor audio-visual quality. For some there may also have been an unconscious urge to stay in a more dulled state rather than face the true reality of the situation. This is in conjunction with immune and endocrine responses that come with survive states. It is suggested that brain fog is an alarm bell that tells us that we are pushing ourselves too hard and need to take off as much time as we can, not something senior clients probably think that they can do.

Bereavement

One of the common symptoms of being bereaved can be tiredness or exhaustion (Sanders, 1992; Stroebe *et al.*, 2001). When my mother died in 2019, despite my work background and training, I was really surprised about just how exhausted I felt. I knew the theory, but I really did not expect to feel *that* tired. I didn't like it, I wanted it to stop. This can be compounded by already feeling depleted due to living alongside someone during the last months and days of their life and the need to look after others who are also bereaved.

It is useful to remember that those who have a member of the family who is very ill may experience anticipatory grief (Nielsen *et al.*, 2016): the grief that someone can experience in anticipation of the loss of a terminally ill person which has many of the same symptoms of grief experienced after a death. One of the symptoms is fatigue, and I would argue that there is an accompanying (di)stress which can lead to a depletion of energy. I experienced anticipatory grief when my mother was in the last few years of her life (she had Alzheimer's for 13 years). I remember that it was not only exhausting but I also think I behaved in a very 'hyper' way on a few social occasions (looking back I think it was inappropriate high energy given the context), trying to prove that I was absolutely fine, when I absolutely wasn't!

Trauma

As detailed in Chapter 1 having a traumatic experience or past trauma can lead to behaviour which may be witnessed and experienced as depleted energy or inappropriate high energy.

Caring for others

This may be stating the obvious but looking after children, in whatever context, can be exhausting. The sleepless nights from having a baby or toddler who hasn't read the baby book that says they should be sleeping through the night right now, or from having the teenager that hasn't come in when they said they would. The constant juggle of childcare, school appointments, school trips, waking at 5am to realise that you haven't made the cake for the school fair (yes, it was going to be flapjack again): this can be tiring stuff.

Our clients may well be caring for elderly parents, for a partner or sibling or a combination of these (throw in the kids too). This can be physically exhausting, time consuming and emotional. In addition, being a carer has been shown to impact health including impaired immune function and poorer health-related behaviours (Umberson and Montez, 2010) which will very likely impact the energy someone has for their work.

To sum up

This chapter has outlined some of the very many influences that may impact the energy of our senior coaching clients. I also believe that this is relevant to employees at other levels in organisations. This knowledge is valuable information for both the coach and the client. Knowing what influences one's energy is useful in itself to heighten awareness but it also allows for appropriate action to be taken if the client so wishes.

References

Adan, A. (2012) 'Cognitive performance and dehydration', *Journal of the American College of Nutrition*, **31**(2), pp. 71–78. Available at: https://doi.org/10.1080/07315724.2012.10720011

Adolf, E.F. (1947) *Physiology of man in the desert*. New York: Interscience.

Arroll, B. and Kendrick, T. (2018) 'Anxiety'. In Gask, L., Kendrick, T., Peveler, R. and Chew-Graham, C.A. (eds.) *Primary care mental health*. Cambridge: Cambridge University Press, pp. 125–135.

Atwater, L. and Carmeli, A. (2009) 'Leader-member exchange, feelings of energy, and involvement in creative work', *The Leadership Quarterly*, **20**(3), pp. 264–275.

Bachkirova, T. and Cox, E. (2007) 'Coaching with emotion in organisations: Investigation of personal theories', *Leadership and Organization Development Journal*, **28**(7), pp. 600–612.

Bargh, J.A. and Morsella, E. (2008) 'The unconscious mind', *Perspectives on Psychological Science*, **3**(1), pp. 73–79.

Baumeister, R.F., Vohs, K.D. and Tice, D.M. (2007) 'The strength model of self-control', *Current Directions in Psychological Science*, **6**(6), pp. 351–355.

Baumeister, R.F., Vohs, K.D., Aaker, J.L. and Garbinsky, E.N. (2013) 'Some key differences between a happy life and a meaningful life', *Journal of Positive Psychology*, **8**(6), pp. 505–516. Available at: https://doi.org/10.1080/17439760.2013.830764

Benton, D. and Young, H.A. (2015) 'Do small differences in hydration status affect mood and mental performance?' *Nutrition Reviews*, **73**(2), pp. 83–96. Available at: https://doi.org/10.1093/nutrit/nuv045

Boyatzis, R., Smith, M. and Blaize, N. (2006) 'Developing sustainable leaders through coaching and compassion', *Academy of Management Learning & Education*, **5**(1), pp. 8–24.

Brandon, J.E. and Loftin, M. (1991) 'Relationship of fitness to depression, state and trait anxiety, internal health, locus of control, and self-control', *Perceptual and Motor Skills*, **73**(2), pp. 563–568.

Bridges, W. (2009) *Managing transitions: Making the most of change*. London: Nicholas Brealey Publishing.

Brown, P.T. and Dzendrowskyj, T. (2018) 'Sorting out an emotional muddle', *Developing Leaders*, **29**(Spring), pp. 26–31.

Brown, P., Kingsley J. and Paterson, S. (2015) *The fear-free organization*. London: Kogan Page.

Brown, P. and Lanz, K. (2019) 'Coaching leaders with neuroscience'. In Passmore, J., Underhill, B.O. and Goldsmith, M. (eds.) *Mastering executive coaching*. Abingdon: Routledge, pp. 226–240.

Brown, P.T., Swart, T. and Meyler. J., (2009) 'Emotional intelligence and the amygdala: Towards the development of the concept of the limbic leader in executive coaching', *NeuroLeadership Journal*, **2**, pp. 67–77.

Butler, G. (1993) 'Definitions of stress', In *Stress management in general practice*. Occasional paper (Royal College of General Practitioners), **61**, pp. iv–42.

Cartwright, S. and Holmes, N. (2006) 'The meaning of work: The challenge or regaining employee engagement and reducing cynicism', *Human Resources Management Review*, **16**(2), pp. 199–208.

Childre, D. and Rozman, D. (2003) *Transforming anger: The HeartMath solution for letting go of rage, frustration, and irritation*. Oakland: New Harbinger Publications.

CIPD (2020) *Embedding new ways of working: Implications for the post-pandemic workplace*. London: Chartered Institute of Personnel and Development.

Cross, R., Baker, W. and Parker, A. (2003) 'What creates energy in organisations', *MIT Sloan Management Review*, **44**(4), pp. 51–56.

Czeisler, C.A. and Fryer, B. (2006) 'Sleep deficit: The performance killer. A conversation with Harvard Medical School Professor Charles A. Czeisler', *Harvard Business Review*, **84**(10), pp. 33–59.

Davenport, S. (2020) *Reboot your brain: Afraid of losing your mind?* Leominster: Orphans Press.

De Bloom, J., Kinnunen, U. and Korpela, K. (2015) 'Recovery processes during and after work: Associations with health, work engagement and job performance', *Journal of Occupational and Environmental Medicine*, **57**(7), pp. 732–743.

Du, J., Huang, J., An, Y. and Xu, W. (2018) 'The relationship between stress and negative emotion: The mediating role of rumination', *Clinical Research and Trials*, **4**(1), pp. 1–5. Available at: https://doi.org/ 10.15761/CRT.1000208

Dutton, J.E. (2003) *Energise your workplace: How to create and sustain high-quality connections at work*. San Francisco: Wiley.

Fritz, C., Lam, C. and Spreitzer, G. (2011) 'It's the little things that matter: An examination of knowledge workers' energy management', *The Academy of Management Perspectives*, **24**(3), pp. 28–139.

Fultz, N.E., Bonmassar, G., Setsompop, K., Stickgold, R.A., Rosen, B.R., Polimeni, J.R. and Lewis, L.D. (2019) 'Coupled electrophysiological, hemodynamic, and cerebrospinal fluid oscillations in human sleep', *Science*, **366**(6454), pp. 628–631. Available at: https://doi.org/ 10.1126/science.aax5440

Gailliot, M.T. and Baumeister, R.F. (2007) 'The physiology of willpower: Linking blood glucose to self-control', *Personality and Social Psychology Review*, **11**(4), pp. 303–327.

Ganio, M.S., Armstrong, L.E., Casa, D.J., McDermott, B.P., Lee, E.C., Yamamoto, L.M., Marzano, S., Lopez, R.M., Jimenez, L., Le Bellego, L., Chevillotte, E. and Lieberman, H.R. (2011) 'Mild dehydration impairs cognitive performance and mood of men', *British Journal of Nutrition*, **106**(10), pp. 1535–1543. Available at: https://doi.org/10.1017/S0007114511002005

Gardner, S. (2003) The unconscious mind'. In Baldwin, T. (ed.) *The Cambridge history of philosophy 1870–1940*. Cambridge, United Kingdom: Cambridge University Press.

Gilbert, P. (2018) 'Introducing compassion-focused therapy', *Advances in Psychiatric Treatment*, **15**(3), pp. 199–208. Available at: https://doi.org/10.1192/apt.bp.107.005264

Goldstein, A.N. and Walker, M.P. (2014) 'The role of sleep in emotional brain function', *Annual Review of Clinical Psychology*, **10**(1), pp. 679–708.

Golomb, B.A., Evans, M.A., White, H.L. and Dimsdale, J.E. (2012) 'Trans Fat consumption and aggression', *PLoS One*, **7**(3). Available at: https://doi.org/10.1371/journal.pone.0032175

Grandey, A.A. (2000) 'Emotion regulation in the workplace: A new way to conceptualize emotional labor', *Journal of Occupational Health Psychology*, **5**(1), pp. 95–110.

Grant, A. (2021) 'There's a name for the blah you're feeling: It's called languishing', *New York Times*, 19 April. Available at: https://www.nytimes.com/2021/04/19/well/mind/covid-mental-health-languishing.html

Hewlin, P.F. (2003) 'And the award for best actor goes to …: Facades of conformity in organizational settings', *Academy of Management Review*, **28**(4), Available at: https://doi.org/10.5465/amr.2003.10899442

Hochschild, A.R. (1979) 'Emotion work, feeling rules, and social structure', *American Journal of Sociology*, **85**(3), pp. 551–575.

Kadzielski, J., McCormick F. and Herndon, J.H. (2015) 'Surgeons' attitudes are associated with reoperation and readmission rates', *Clinical Orthopaedics and Related Research*, **473**(5), pp. 1544–1551.

Keyes, C.L.M. (2002) 'The mental health continuum: From languishing to flourishing in life', *Journal of Health and Social Behavior*, **43**(2), pp. 207–222. Available at: https://doi.org/10.2307/3090197

Kim, S., Park, Y. and Niu, Q. (2017) 'Micro-break activities at work to recover from daily work demands', *Journal of Organizational Behavior*, **38**(1), pp. 28–44.

Kinnunen, U., Feldt, T., de Bloom. J. and Korpela, K. (2015) 'Patterns of daily energy management at work: Relations to employee well-being and job characteristics', *International Archives of Occupational and Environmental Health*, **88**(8), pp. 1077–1086. Available at: https://doi.org/10.1007/s00420-015-1039-9

Kline, N. (2020) *The promise that changes everything: I won't interrupt you*. London: Penguin Random House.

Kuhnel, J., Zacher, H., de Bloom, J. and Bledow, R. (2017) 'Take a break! Benefits of sleep and short breaks for daily work engagement', *European Journal of Work and Organizational Psychology*, **26**(4), pp. 481–491.

Kulinski, J.P., Khera, A., Ayers, C.R., Das, S.R., de Lemos, J.A., Blair, S.N. and Berry, J.D. (2014) 'Association between cardiorespiratory fitness and accelerometer-derived physical activity and sedentary time in the general population', *Mayo Clinic Proceedings*, **89**(8), pp. 1063–1071. Available at: https://doi.org/10.1016/j.mayocp.2014.04.019

Kupriyanov, R. and Zhdanov, R. (2014) 'The eustress concept: Problems and outlooks', *World Journal of Medical Sciences*, **11**(2), pp. 179–185.

Kushlev, K. and Dunn, E.W. (2015) 'Checking email less frequently reduces stress', *Computers in Behaviour*, **43**, pp. 220–228.

Langle, A. (2003) 'Burnout: Existential meaning and possibilities of prevention', *European Psychotherapy*, **4**(1), pp. 107–121.

Lanz, K. and Brown. P.T. (2020) *All the brains in the business: The engendered brain in the 21st Century organisation*. Switzerland: Palgrave Macmillan.

Lazarus, R.S. and Folkman, S. (1984) *Stress, appraisal and coping*. New York: Springer.

Lee, R.T., Ashforth, B.E. and Blake, E. (1996) 'A meta-analytic examination of the correlates of the three dimensions of job burnout', *Journal of Applied Psychology*, **81**(2), pp. 123–133.

Leger, D., Richard, J., Collin, O., Sauvet, F. and Faraut, B. (2020) 'Napping and weekend catch-up sleep do not fully compensate for high rates of sleep debt and short sleep at a population level', *Sleep Medicine*, **74**, pp. 278–288.

Li, J., Burch, T.C. and Lee, T.W. (2017) 'Intra-individual variability in job complexity over time: Examining the effect of job complexity trajectory on employee job strain', *Journal of Organizational Behavior*, **38**(5), pp. 671–691.

Loehr, J. and Schwartz, T. (2003) *The power of full engagement: Managing energy, not time, is the key to high performance and personal renewal*. New York: Free Press.

Lovelace, K.J., Manz, C.C. and Alves, J.C. (2007) 'Work stress and leadership development. The role of self-leadership, shared leadership, physical fitness and flow in managing demands and increasing job control', *Human Resource Management Review*, **17**(4), pp. 374–387.

Marcus, S.M., Flynn, H.A., Blow, F.C. and Barry, K.L. (2003) 'Depressive symptoms among pregnant women screened in obstetric settings', *Journal of Women's Health*, **12**(4), pp. 373–380.

Maslach, C., Schaufeli, W.B. and Leiter, M.P. (2001) 'Job burnout', *Annual Review of Psychology*, **52**, pp. 397–422.

McClelland, D.C. (1985). 'How motives, skills, and values determine what people do', *American Psychologist*, **40**(7), pp. 812–825. Available at: https://doi.org/10.1037/0003-066X.40.7.812

Michaud, K., Matheson, K., Kelly, O. and Anisman, H. (2008) 'Impact of stressors in a natural context on release of cortisol in healthy adult humans:

A metaanalysis', *Stress*, **11**(3), pp. 177–197. Available at: https://doi.org/10.1080/10253890701727874

Microsoft (2021) *Research proves your brain needs breaks*. WTI Pulse Report. Available at: http://www.microsoft.com/en-us/worklab/work-trend-index/brain-research#:~:text=In%20our%20latest%20study%20of,a%20simple%20remedy%E2%80%94short%20breaks

Nader, K., Schafe G.E. and Le Doux, J.E. (2000) 'Fear memories require protein synthesis in the amygdala for reconsolidation after retrieval', *Nature*, 406, pp. 722–726 Available at: https://doi.org/10.1038/35021052

Nakamura, J. and Csikszentmihalyi, M. (2009) 'Flow theory and research'. In Snyder, C.R. and Lopez, S.J. (eds.) *Oxford handbook of positive psychology*. New York: Oxford University Press, pp. 195.

Nestor, J. (2020) *Breath: The new science of a lost art*. UK: Penguin Life.

NICE (2020) *Tiredness/fatigue in adults*. Available at: https://cks.nice.org.uk/topics/tiredness-fatigue-in-adults

Nielsen, M.K., Neergaard, M.A., Jensen, A.B., Bro, F. and Guldin, M.B. (2016) 'Do we need to change our understanding of anticipatory grief in caregivers? A systematic review of caregiver studies during end-of-life caregiving and bereavement', *Clinical Psychology Review*, **44**(March), pp. 75–93.

Olsen, O.K., Pallesen, S., Torsheim, T. and Espevik, R. (2016) 'The effect of sleep deprivation on leadership behaviour in military officers: An experimental study', *Journal of Sleep Research* **25**(6), pp. 683–689.

Parfitt, G. and Gledhill, C. (2004) 'The effect of choice of exercise mode on psychological responses', *Psychology of Sport and Exercise*, **5**(2), pp. 111–117.

Parker, S.L., Zacher, H., de Bloom, J., Verton, M. and Lentink, C.R. (2017) 'Daily use of energy management strategies and occupational well-being: The moderating role of job demands', *Frontiers in Psychology*, **8**, pp. 1–12. Available at: https://doi.org/10.3389/fpsyg.2017.01477

Parry, D., Oeppen, R.S., Gass, H. and Brennan, P.A. (2017) 'Impact of hydration and nutrition on personal performance in the clinical workplace', *British Journal of Oral and Maxillofacial Surgery*, **55**(10), pp. 995–998.

Parry, D.A., Oeppen, R.S., Amin, M.S.A. and Brennan, P.A. (2018) 'Sleep: its importance and the effects of deprivation on surgeons and other healthcare professionals', *British Journal of Oral and Maxillofacial Surgery*, **56**(8), pp. 663–666.

Porges, S.W. (2020) 'The COVID-19 Pandemic is a paradoxical challenge to our nervous system: A polyvagal perspective', *Clinical Neuropsychiatry*, **17**(2), pp. 135–138.

Quinn, R.W., Spreitzer, G.M. and Lam, C.F. (2012) 'Building a sustainable model of human energy in organizations: Exploring the critical role of resources', *The Academy of Management Annals*, **6**(1), pp. 337–396.

Riethof, B., Bob, P., Laker, M., Varakova, K., Jiraskova, T. and Raboch, J. (2019) 'Burnout syndrome and logotherapy: Logotherapy as useful conceptual framework for explanation and prevention of burnout', *Frontiers in Psychiatry*, **10**, pp. 1–8. Available at: https://doi.org/10.3389/fpsyt.2019.00382

Rock, D. (2008) 'SCARF: A brain-based model for collaborating with and influencing others', *NeuroLeadership Journal*, **1**, pp. 1–9.

Rothbard, N.P., Phillips, K.W. and Dumas, T.L. (2005) 'Managing multiple roles: Work-family policies and individuals' desires for segmentation', *Organization Science*, **16**(3), pp. 243–258. Available at: https://doi.org/10.1287/orsc.1050.0124

Sanches, I., Teixeira, F., dos Santos, J.M. and Ferreira, A.J. (2015) 'Effects of acute sleep deprivation resulting from night shift work on young doctors', *Acta Medica Portuguesa*, **28**(4), pp. 457–462.

Sanders, C.M. (1992) *Surviving grief: And learning to live again.* Canada: Wiley.

Sarner, M. (2021) 'Brain fog: how trauma, uncertainty and isolation have affected our minds and memory', *The Guardian*, 14 April. Available at: https://www.theguardian.com/lifeandstyle/2021/apr/14/brain-fog-how-trauma-uncertainty-andisolation-have-affected-our-minds-and-memory

Schippers, M.C. and Hogenes, R. (2011) 'Energy management of people in organizations: A review and research agenda', *Journal of Business and Psychology*, **26**(193), pp. 193–203. Available at: https://doi.org/10.1007/s10869-011-9217-6

Shiota, M.N., Neufeld, S.L., Yeung, W.H., Moser, S.E. and Perea, E.F. (2011) 'Feeling good: Autonomic nervous system responding in five positive emotions', *Emotion*, **11**(6), pp. 1368–1378. Available at: https://doi.org/10.1037/a0024278

Sonnentag, S., Binnewies, C. and Mojza, E.J. (2008) '"Did you have a nice evening?" A day-level study on recovery experiences, sleep and affect', *Journal of Applied Psychology*, **93**(3), pp. 674–684.

Sonnentag, S., Binnewies, C. and Mojza, E.J. (2010) 'Staying well and engaged when demands are high: The role of psychological detachment', *Journal of Applied Psychology*, **95**(5), pp. 965–976.

Soon, C.S., Brass, M., Jochen Heinze, H. and Haynes, J.D. (2008) 'Unconscious determinants of free decisions in the human brain', *Nature Neuroscience*, **11**(5) pp. 543–545.

Stokes, J. and Jolly, R. (2014) 'Executive and leadership coaching'. In Cox, E., Bachkirova, T. and Clutterbuck, D. (eds.) *The complete handbook of coaching*, 2nd edn. London: Sage, pp. 244–255.

Stone, L. (2007) 'The Harvard Business Review list of breakthrough ideas for 2007: Living with Continuous Partial Attention', *Harvard Business Review*, **85**(2), pp. 28–29.

Stroebe, M.S., Hansson, R.O., Stroebe, W. and Schut, H. (2001) 'Introduction: Concepts and issues in contemporary research on bereavement'. In Stroebe, M.S., Hansson, R.O., Stroebe, W. and Schut, H. (eds.) *Handbook of bereavement research: Consequences, coping, and care.* Washington D.C: American Psychological Association, pp. 3–22.

Swart, T., Chisholm, K. and Brown, P. (2015) *Neuroscience for leadership: Harnessing the brain gain advantage.* Basingstoke: Palgrave Macmillan.

Umberson, D. and Montez, J.K. (2010) 'Social relationships and health: A flashpoint for health policy', *Journal of Health and Social Behavior*, **51**(Suppl), pp. 54–66.

Vohs, K.D., Baumeister, R.F., Schmeichel, B.J., Twenge, J.M., Nelson, N.M. and Tice, D.M. (2014) 'Making choices impairs subsequent self-control: A limited resource account of decision making, self-regulation, and active initiative', *Motivation Science*, **1**(S), pp. 19–42.

Watkins, A. (2014) *Coherence: The secret science of brilliant leadership.* London: Kogan Page.

White, B.A., Horwath, C.C. and Conner, T.S. (2013) 'Many apples a day keep the blues away: Daily experiences of negative and positive affect and food consumption in young adults', *British Journal of Health Psychology*, **18**(4), pp. 782–798.

Xueming, L., Kanuri, V.K. and Andrews, M. (2013) 'Long CEO tenure can hurt performance', *Harvard Business Review*, **91**(3), p. 26.

Zakerimoghadam, M., Marzieh, S., Anoushiravan, K. and Tavasoli, K.H. (2006) 'The effect of breathing exercises on fatigue level of COPD patients', *Hayat*, **12**(3), pp. 17–25.

3
Why address energy and the role of the executive coach in doing so

THIS CHAPTER CONSIDERS WHY having Optimal Energy® is important for senior executives in order for them to meet the many demands of their working life and life outside of work. It then moves on to review the benefits of consciously considering energy levels and the role of the coach in enabling clients to do so. All the quotes in this chapter are made by fellow executive coaches and reproduced with their permission.

Why optimal energy is important for the performance of senior executives

Let's consider what is expected of those in senior positions within organisations. This may be in a corporate environment, but also in environments which are underfunded or even dangerous and where people are making life and death decisions such as in hospitals. Senior people have responsibility for any number of the functions listed below (in no order of priority) and are expected to:

- Set and communicate vision and strategic direction for the organisation
- Have strategic flexibility and manage shifting priorities
- Design and manage organisational change and restructuring, downsizing and challenging the status quo
- Drive revenue and profit, oversee planning and budgets
- Manage systemic shocks to the business, such as the COVID-19 pandemic, which may require restructuring of the business and remotivating sometimes exhausted or furloughed staff at the same time as seeing the creative opportunities for reinvention and presenting new vision
- Develop what the organisation offers
- Create alignment
- Ensure that diversity/difference within the workforce is recognised, managed and enhanced, often in global organisations

- Address environmental issues, environmental impact, drive their business to be carbon neutral and for some, hopefully many, have a regenerative focus
- Drive increasing profitability and/or efficiency in a highly competitive market, often with diminishing resources and increasing costs
- Ensure delivery of organisational goals
- Ensure governance is effective
- Manage risk, including risk arising from global recession and global health crises
- Understand wider systems and think and function systemically, being aware of organisational habits and set patterns
- Ensure that performance and talent is managed
- Be in touch with staff at all levels of the organisation
- Be creative, innovative and have fresh perspectives, and be able to problem solve
- Be self-motivated and engaged
- Have self-control
- Exhibit confidence
- Be resilient
- Be engaging, inspiring and maintain commitment
- Make great presentations within the organisation and externally
- Manage the relationship with external providers and clients
- Connect with others, forming good and effective relationships with those senior to them, peers and people they manage
- Be present and listen
- Lead and manage direct reports, considering their well-being, development and motivation
- Ensure that the working environment is one people feel safe to work in
- Build trust in the organisation, both personally and encourage this in teams
- Develop personally and maybe engage in their own coaching, putting new ideas into practice
- Remember their own well-being
- Progress within the organisation and manage their career

All of these complex functions take place against a backdrop of ever-shifting organisational and global developments and an immensely and often increasingly demanding world both work-wise and out of work where the individual may also be expected to be a great parent, partner, be supportive to aging parents and want to have a personal life.

How can you do this without having enough energy?

Having optimal energy has been shown to have numerous benefits. For example, it allows for: the maintenance of behaviour that leads to high performance and productivity (Quinn, Spreitzer and Lam, 2012; Parker *et al.*, 2017); engagement with work (Loehr and Schwartz, 2003; Brown, Swart and Chisholm, 2015); the ability to inspire, have a positive impact on and energise others (Cross and Parker, 2004; Watkins, 2014) and resilience. My research indicated that being appropriately energised influences the ability to connect well with others, be truly engaged with the other person, present and able to listen. In addition, peer-reviewed research has shown that the maintenance of optimal energy for senior executives is positively related to: career success, satisfaction and life satisfaction (Baruch, Grimland and Vigoda-Gadot, 2014); health and well-being at work (Quinn, Spreitzer and Lam, 2012; Parker *et al.*, 2017) and higher levels of creativity (Atwater and Carmeli, 2009).

The arguments for being conscious of energy and taking action to manage it

In these demanding environments the individual will benefit from having, and organisations will need their leaders to have, optimal energy levels in order to be able to carry out their day-to-day tasks and meet any variety of the expectations listed above. Optimal energy refers to having the right amount of energy for what you are trying to do and achieve at a given time. In addition, energy levels need to be sustainable: as one of my research partners said, "if we're in it for the long haul, then it's got to be sustainable. Everybody can burn like a 'supernova' but it doesn't last very long". But to qualify this, I am writing about having optimal energy some of the time, it is an unrealistic expectation that it will be all of the time, in fact I suggest that the pressure of this would be detrimental in itself.

It has been argued that conscious energy self-management is an underlying skill of leadership (Watkins, 2014). Skilful management of energy means knowing what you need with regard to energy at a given time, recognising when your energy levels are optimal, lacking, and not appropriate and understanding what you personally need to do to address this.

I need to consciously be aware of how I expend the energy that I have. Because even though at certain stages in life it feels like it's boundless and limitless, it's not. So it has to be conscious because throughout life there will be peaks and troughs in the need for us to expend energy and if I'm not conscious of it then I can lead myself into all sorts of problems because I become depleted to the point where I break down. There's probably something on the other side of that scale, you know, where I become so excitable and buzzed about something that I become something else. I become, maybe to the world's eye, some kind of

deranged fool. So there is something about making it conscious I think.
(Executive Coach speaking personally)

Intentional consideration of, and acting to address, energy and self-care in this context can have massive value for the individual rather than being a cosy 'add-on' to their agenda because there are so many benefits to having optimal energy.

> *My client had a chronically ill parent, and was needed for the emotional support of both parents, plus two young children. She realised in coaching that she had to manage her energy very carefully. She negotiated a reduction in workload (for a short period of time) and consciously took good care of herself in order to be sufficiently energised to cope with all the demands being made of her. She realised that she had been pushing herself harder and harder trying to prove to everyone that she was fine. But in the end this wasn't working and she was exhausted. We worked on her being able to recognise when her energy levels were dipping or extremely depleted and become very aware of what was going to be re-energising for her and to act on this. She made sure that she ate well, stayed hydrated, did yoga, meditated, did a bit of exercise and sought support from friends. I would say that she was skilful in how she did this and this came out of true awareness of her energy levels.*

The bottom line is that there are proven benefits to having optimal and appropriate energy levels and however good an individual's work-related intentions are, if they are not appropriately energised to act on them they are less likely to succeed. There are also negative impacts of being inappropriately energised and taking conscious action to address energy can help to negate these. Some may argue that it is the ethical duty of senior people to address these risks, because poor decisions, behaviour and relationships could be the potential result.

The negative impact of having depleted energy at work

Having depleted energy can impact a person's performance at work in many ways. For example, they may:

- Be anxious, fearful and angry
- Be disassociated from, and unable to acknowledge, their own feelings and emotions (Loehr, 2007)
- Come across as irritable with those around them, maybe becoming disengaged from others, both colleagues and family
- Have little passion for what they are doing and low motivation, maybe having difficulty completing tasks
- Find it more difficult to take risks and be courageous, for example, less likely to have tough conversations with

colleagues: this may be partly due to feeling fatigued and also because they fear that this might tire them further

- And their cognitive functioning can be negatively affected in a number of ways, for example, impacting their ability to focus; process ideas; have a vision and see the bigger picture; have innovative thoughts and new insight and be able to accept new ideas and concepts from others

So I think there's that sense of 'I'm feeling tired' and 'I've got to override this tiredness. I've actually got to keep going because I've got this deadline and I've got this in-tray and I've got ten meetings to get through before teatime. I cannot actually give in to the fact that my body isn't feeling great, even though this might mean that I'm not doing great work. It might even mean that I'm substituting inefficiency for effectiveness. And it might be that I'm doing rubbish work and causing rework. And also that I am causing potential damage and I am becoming toxic'.

Their resilience, their capacity to stop, step back and think is severely hampered if their energy levels are depleted. So it's enormous. It's huge.

Depleted energy over a long period of time can lead to exhaustion with resultant demotivation, maybe resulting in a need to take time out or a desire to leave the organisation. You may recall the former chief executive of Lloyds Banking Group, António Horta-Osório, taking two months off due to sleep deprivation and fatigue caused by workload concerns saying that it was like "getting close to the end of your battery" (Treanor, 2011).

The very top of project management is vicious. You won't survive if you don't have enough energy. You just won't survive. And I've seen several go under. A while ago someone asked me to see a guy who was struggling. He sat there and the first thing he said to me was, "I've just had a hundred and eighty emails in the last five minutes". And I said to him, "You've got to the level of counting emails coming in?" That is all he had done. I thought, he's finished. And he was: he never came in to work again.

The negative impact of inappropriate high energy

Inappropriate high energy is also very likely to be detrimental, for example, it may result in:

- Cognitive impacts such as affecting the ability to think clearly and unwillingness to accept new creativity from others

- An impact on mood, for example, leading to overenthusiasm, irritability or anger
- The individual being so driven that they do not make time for rest and recreation
- A negative effect on the ability to form relationships with colleagues
- A lack of empathy for others
- A lack of awareness, or care, as to how they are being perceived with a 'like it or lump it' mentality
- A negative impact on an individual's ability to lead, inspire, take people with them and set a pace that others can keep up with
- An impact on others, for example, Childre and Rozman (2003) propose that when someone is angry others might find them alarming or actually frightening
- Stress within the organisation, not just to individuals, due to being overly enthused and/or angry
- A resultant destructive impact on organisational culture

I remember coaching somebody who had very, very high energy and actually it caused enormous stress in the team. You know, that person who's always on your back and actually is disempowering because their presence is so dominant.

… someone who gets there at 6.30 am in the morning and works until 10.30 pm at night. It sets an appalling culture. People who have endless amounts of energy: the Maggie Thatchers of this world. I used to work with a guy who worked in three time zones. And he had three secretaries. Drove everybody bonkers. He had so much energy, he was far too perfect. So I think that impacts.

One interesting take on those who live their working lives exhibiting inappropriate high energy a lot of the time is the theory of living 'fast'. Carter (2020) describes the risks of living fast rather than 'slow' in the context of the hormones oxytocin and vasopressin, which she says work not alone but together, a 'dynamic dance' between love/connection and fear/defence. When operating a fast lifestyle, commonly seen in senior executives, there is a reliance on vasopressin which facilitates mobilisation which is obviously very useful in the workplace. Despite there being benefits when vasopressin is dominant and oxytocin deficient, survival strategies come into play: defence (against real or imagined threat) and aggression; increased likelihood of avoidant social behaviours which are defensive of self and others and a reduced likelihood for adaptive learning including adaptation to changes in the environment. She suggests that the resultant likely increase in anxiety and fear, with accompanying cardiovascular arousal and a greater likelihood for inflammation, has long-term implications for chronic disease. In addition, those in this state usually believe in the survival of the fittest, being the strongest and most competitive, and crave resources often in the form of money. At the same time the individual will be less able to replenish their energetic resources when in this fast state of threat unlike those in a slow state. Whereas when in a slower mode the dominant hormone of the two is oxytocin which allows for strategies of cooperation, positive social behaviours, cognitive adaptation and learning and reduced anxiety and fear. Oxytocin has many benefits including being critical to having a sense of safety and coping with stress. It is also an underlying central feature of social behaviour, aids complex cognition, and has positive effects on the ability to relax and restore. There is a positive impact on health including the potential reduction of inflammation and on immune system function, healing and longevity.

Carter also suggests that living fast can be due to lifestyle, prolonged trauma, or is a reaction to poor attachment or a learnt behaviour in childhood sometimes because of over-critical parenting. Some people only live fast because it keeps them from being in a vulnerable state. The inability to co-regulate with others means that the person never really feels safe and also cannot make the world better for others. Living in a slow way actually challenges these individuals' definition of success, whereas Carter believes that ultimately success actually comes from co-regulation with others which fulfils our biological imperative. She stresses that if we don't fulfil our biological imperative we are not successful.

> *Most of the bad decisions I've seen made are by overly highly energised people who are firefighting and they've got their underpants out over their trousers and think 'I'm going to fix it because I'm high energy and I can put the fire out'. Well, who bloody started the fire in the first place? The person who was too energetic to get the project started properly.*

> *I got the shock of my life because my God, this guy is smack in your face with a level of energy where he's just completely going to destroy his company if he's not careful. His energy is massively destructive. Not for him, for his organisation and for some of the people in his organisation. And he sort of knows it is. He's totally selfish: it's his way. Other people have just got to cope with him. He's got such a high energy level, he doesn't want to lose it and he thoroughly enjoys it. He was almost going to explode in front of me. It's amazing. And that's terribly destructive because he has no empathy whatsoever. He sees his energy as good. When actually, for other people it isn't good and he isn't getting the best out of his people. They are actually pissed off with him.*

One coach talked about working with a newly appointed CEO who was having a negative impact on other people. *He's trying to get everyone to run a marathon in under four hours: which he could do. And most of them couldn't run fifty yards. He is so energised and so excited by new opportunities he's driving people nuts.*

Coping strategies are not always constructive and can be damaging

In reality, most senior people are rushed off their feet. They are constantly in meetings with very little time to do their actual work, bombarded by emails and spending rather too much time checking their phones. So how do they cope? I have witnessed coping strategies such as using caffeinated drinks (I had one client who drank only caffeinated diet cola all day to get through a gruelling schedule); using alcohol to calm down in the evening; taking sleeping pills to get to sleep when their mind is still racing at bedtime and other methods to whip the metaphorical racehorse running along panting to a finish line which is nowhere in sight. For many this is not sustainable and although most are aware that this is the case, it seems that they carry on, hoping that they will be fine and at some point get to the finishing line whatever that might be for them.

Why addressing energy is the role of the coach

So far in this chapter, I have illustrated why it is important for executives to have optimal energy at a given time to meet the expectations made of them and how suboptimal energy can be detrimental, as are some coping strategies. The fact that it is important for our clients to have optimal energy as much as possible is a pretty strong argument for addressing this in coaching in itself but the argument can be further supported by considering the relevance of this work to the generic aims of coaching and coaching competencies.

How coaching for optimal energy relates to the generic aims of coaching

Despite carrying out an extensive search I found no coaching research literature which focuses on the role of the coach in this context or on what interventions might be appropriate. This is despite strategies to address energy, identified in other research fields, being shown to be useful in enhancing performance and well-being, which is what coaches in part seek to do (Passmore, 2007; O'Connor and Cavanagh, 2013). As a result, the second objective for my research was to investigate whether executive coaches have a role in helping clients address their energy. The conclusion reached was that working with energy levels can play a valid part of the coach's role in being alongside the client as they deepen their understanding of their emotions, behaviour and whatever else they chose to focus on – if it is appropriate for the client at that time.

If we look at some of the generic aims of coaching mentioned in the literature we can see how enabling clients to manage their energy fits into many of the categories. For example, coaching aims to enable clients to:

- Become more self-aware (Stokes and Jolly, 2014). Addressing energy further enables clients to increase their self-understanding, helping clients to become more aware of their 'behaviour, thoughts and feelings': to develop 'psychological mindedness' (Bluckert, 2006)
- Develop and function more effectively (Bachkirova, 2009) and increase awareness of what is getting in the way of performance and change (Kegan and Lahey, 2009). The coach can work with the client to identify when having depleted or inappropriate high energy is blocking them from fulfilling their potential and from being able to action their coaching. I have noticed several clients in the past have engaged with their coaching with enthusiasm in sessions and gone away having both explored the issues they want to address and decided upon some actions that they want to take. However, on returning to the next session it has become apparent that something is getting in the way of them acting: I started to realise that they just didn't have the energy to do so
- Cope with the demands made of them at work and out of work (Kauffman, Joseph and Scoular, 2015; Bachkirova and Borrington, 2020). Bachkirova and Borrington suggest that this might be the most appropriate aim of coaching particularly with the current challenges that we all face in the world at the moment: 'promoting our ability to cope with adversity prompts the development of new capacities and makes substantive contributions to building the levels of confidence and adaptability to deal with those difficulties that present themselves in both our working and our personal lives' (Bachkirova and Borrington, 2020, p. 22). Coaches can help clients identify and meet demands, exploring the sustainability of their current behaviour and workload, within the context of having optimal energy
- Engage in holistic reflection (Schon, 1983): connecting emotional, cognitive and physical aspects of the client (Lee, 2014). Siegel (2017) writes that coaching and other helping relationships can help someone with the innate human process of developing integration (the state of mind that exists between rigidity, being stuck in patterns of thinking and behaviour, and

chaos, when life is unpredictable, explosive and at times distressing). Such integration in turn leads to more energy as well as flexibility, stability and resilience. This can be done by the practitioner helping the client to link their differentiated parts by taking into account different streams of awareness (sensations; images; feelings and thoughts). Such holistic reflection can be addressed in, and be an outcome of, coaching about energy

- Enhance their well-being, as mentioned above (Passmore, 2007; O'Connor and Cavanagh, 2013). As well as addressing energy in the daily or weekly work context, coaching which addresses energy may enable the client to take actions which prevent ill health in the long term

- Educate and impart useful information to clients. Some authors suggest that humans often fail to take into account the importance of energy (Loehr and Schwartz, 2003) and that it is usually ignored (Brown and Brown, 2012). Giving an overview of the concept of energy, what influences it, the importance of having optimal energy, and the risks associated with depleted and inappropriately high energy, plus how optimal energy can be achieved, is useful information that can be given to clients

Lastly, a great benefit of coaching for many clients is the experience of the coaching relationship itself. Specifically relating to this context, a relationship with a compassionate coach has been shown to lead to a state of positive emotional arousal (Boyatzis, Smith and Beveridge, 2012) which in turn can result in energetic activation. Some of the coaches I interviewed talked about clients reporting that they felt more energised and uplifted as a result of coaching, one saying that they saw themselves as a "battery recharger". My own experience of coaching supervision is that I can enter the session feeling fatigued and come out far more energised, having had the chance to explore both client work and personal issues in a relationship where I have felt truly listened to and understood. My work with my supervisor can motivate me, enable me to focus and result in me having the energy needed to address intended actions after a session.

Link to coaching competencies

Working with client energy aligns with the coaching competencies outlined by both the International Coach Federation (ICF) and the European Mentoring and Coaching Council (EMCC). The revised ICF competencies (2019) specifically mention energy, requiring that a coach 'notices, acknowledges and explores the client's emotions, energy shifts, non-verbal cues or other behaviours'. Working with a client's energy fits in with many of the other ICF and EMCC (2015) competencies, where the latter is concerned particularly for senior and master practitioners. For example, a coach doing this work is showing concern for a client's welfare and fully demonstrates the competencies relating to: being attentive to the full sensory range of the client's communication, their emotions, language and physical expression; encouraging clients to explore and go beyond the current thinking by evoking awareness, sharing insight and noticing trends and helping them make connections and see different interrelated factors that affect their behaviour and emotion. It also helps clients identify barriers to action.

If organisations don't take this seriously the coach will need to

In my experience, little, if any, time or attention is taken by those with organisational responsibility to address energy and consider how employees, and in this context senior leaders, are going to meet the demands made on them with optimal or at least sufficient energy. Nor, to encourage employees to have personal awareness as to whether the energy they currently have is appropriate. As Lanz and Brown point out, in organisations generally 'there has been a great deal about how to measure performance, but nothing to balance that on how to conserve, renew, or even create the energy that would be appropriate to the performance demands' (Lanz and Brown, 2020, p. 117). This is despite, according to a GALLUP survey, Millennials and Generation Z employees expecting that their employers will prioritise looking after their well-being (Mann and Adkins, 2017). So, if organisations and our clients aren't taking action to address energy then the starting point may well need to be with the coach.

Better outcomes for coaching

Most of us who coach senior executives know that they bring a whole range of issues to coaching and have their own expectations for what will constitute efficacy. The sponsor representing the organisation paying the bill will also have expectations regarding the specific outcomes of coaching that will be indicative of success. Working with energy is very unlikely to replace the overall agenda for coaching (although at times it may if very problematic), it is more likely to underpin it. As well as identifying when a client's energy levels are influencing their personal efficacy, working in this way can identify potential and actual barriers to the success of the coaching and will give the coach a more complete picture of what is going on for their client. This will in turn enhance the efficacy of the coaching and ensure the fulfilment of the expectations of both client and sponsor. Clients are very likely to have better outcomes from their coaching as a result.

References

Atwater, L. and Carmeli, A. (2009) 'Leader-member exchange, feelings of energy, and involvement in creative work', *The Leadership Quarterly*, **20**(3), pp. 264–275.

Bachkirova, T. (2009) 'Cognitive-developmental approach to coaching: an interview with Robert Kegan', *Coaching: An International Journal of Theory, Research and Practice*, **2**(1), pp. 10–22. Available at: https://doi.org/10.1080/17521880802645951

Bachkirova, T. and Borrington, S. (2020) 'Beautiful ideas that can make us ill: Implications for coaching', *Philosophy of Coaching: An International Journal*, **5**(1), pp. 9–30. Available at: https://doi.org/10.22316/poc/05.1.03

Baruch, Y., Grimland, S. and Vigoda-Gadot, E. (2014) 'Professional vitality and career success: Mediation, age and outcomes', *European Management Journal*, **32**(3), pp. 518–527.

Bluckert, P. (2006) *Psychological dimensions of executive coaching*. Maidenhead, UK: Open University Press.

Boyatzis, R.E., Smith, M.L. and Beveridge, A.J. (2012) 'Coaching with compassion: Inspiring health, well-being, and development in organizations', *The Journal of Applied Behavioral Science*, **49**(2), pp. 153–178. Available at: https://doi.org/10.1177/0021886312462236

Brown, P. and Brown, V. (2012) *Neuropsychology for coaches: Understanding the basics*. Maidenhead: Open University Press.

Brown, P., Swart, T. and Chisholm, K. (2015) *Neuroscience for leadership: Harnessing the brain gain advantage*. Basingstoke: Palgrave Macmillan.

Carter, S. (2020) *Understanding Reactions to the COVID-19 Pandemic: Insights from the Polyvagal Theory and the Oxytocin Hypothesis* [webinar]. CONFER. 18 July 2020. https://www.conferonline.org/on-demand-events/vagus.html

Childre, D. and Rozman, D. (2003) *Transforming anger: The HeartMath solution for letting go of rage, frustration, and irritation*. Oakland: New Harbinger Publications.

Cross, R. and Parker, A. (2004) 'Charged up: Creating energy in organizations', *Journal of Organizational Excellence*, **23**(4), pp. 3–14.

EMCC (2015) *EMCC competence framework v2*. Available at: https://www.emccglobal.org/wp-content/uploads/2018/10/EMCC-competences-framework-v2EN.pdf

ICF (2019) *ICF core competencies*. Available at: https://coachingfederation.org/corecompetencies

Kauffman, C., Joseph, S. and Scoular, A. (2015) 'Leadership coaching and positive psychology'. In Joseph, S. (ed.) *Positive psychology in practice: Promoting human flourishing in work, health, education and everyday life*, 2nd edn. Hoboken, N.J.: Wiley, pp. 377–390.

Kegan, R. and Lahey, L.L. (2009) *Immunity to change: How to overcome it and unlock the potential in yourself and your organisation*. Boston, Massachusetts: Harvard Business Press.

Lanz, K. and Brown. P.T. (2020) *All the brains in the business: The engendered brain in the 21st Century organisation*. Switzerland: Palgrave Macmillan.

Lee, G. (2014) 'The psychodynamic approach to coaching'. In Cox, E., Bachkirova, T. and Clutterbuck, D. (eds.) *The complete handbook of coaching*, 2nd edn. London: Sage, pp. 21–33.

Loehr, J. and Schwartz, T. (2003) *The power of full engagement: Managing energy, not time, is the key to high performance and personal renewal*. New York: Free Press.

Loehr, J. (2007) *The power of story: Change your story, change your destiny in business and in life*. New York: Simon and Schuster.

Mann, A. and Adkins, A. (2017) 'What star employees want', *GALLUP Workplace*, 8 March. Available at: https://www.gallup.com/workplace/231767/star-employees.aspx

O'Connor, S. and Cavanagh, M. (2013) 'The coaching ripple effect: The effects of developmental coaching on wellbeing across organizational networks', *Psychology of Well-being, Theory, Research and Practice*, **3**(1), pp. 1–23.

Parker, S.L., Zacher, H., de Bloom, J., Verton, T.M. and Lentink, C.R. (2017) 'Daily use of energy management strategies and occupational well-being: The moderating role of job demands', *Frontiers in Psychology*, **8**, pp. 1–12. Available at: https://doi.org/10.3389/fpsyg.2017

Passmore, J. (2007) 'An integrative model for executive coaching', *Consulting Psychology Journal: Practice and Research*, **59**(1), pp. 68–78.

Quinn, R.W., Spreitzer, G.M. and Lam, C.F. (2012) 'Building a sustainable model of human energy in organizations: Exploring the critical role of resources', *The Academy of Management Annals*, **6**(1), pp. 337–396.

Schon, D. (1983). *The reflective practitioner: How professionals think in action*. US: Basic Books Ltd.

Siegel, D.J. (2017) *Mind: A journey to the heart of being human*. New York: Norton.

Stokes, J. and Jolly, R. (2014) 'Executive and leadership coaching'. In Cox, E., Bachkirova, T. and Clutterbuck, D. (eds.) *The complete handbook of coaching*, 2nd edn. London: SAGE, pp. 244–255.

Treanor, J. (2011) 'Lloyds chief Horta-Osório takes time off with fatigue', *The Guardian*, 2 November. Available at: https://www.theguardian.com/business/2011/nov/02/lloyds-chief-leave-absence-stress

Watkins, A. (2014) *Coherence: The secret science of brilliant leadership*. London: Kogan Page.

4

The journey towards a holistic way of addressing energy with the client

So FAR I HAVE WRITTEN ABOUT the concept of energy, how it manifests and what may influence the energy of senior executives. I have also made the argument for why this needs to be addressed and the role of the executive coach in doing so. This chapter considers the steps coaches can take to assess whether to address energy with a client and how to enable the client to design a holistic, personal approach to working towards having optimal energy levels as much as is possible, practical and manageable in their working life. An overall picture of potential interventions, actions and strategies will be given in this chapter and the rest of the book is devoted to exploring these in further detail. As I stated in the preface, the focus of this book is on executive coaching, however, what is written in this chapter is relevant to all types of coaching, to coach supervision and for others who may want to address energy with their clients in one-to-one and group work. As in the other chapters, all the quotes in this chapter are made by fellow executive coaches and reproduced with their permission.

As far as is possible, what I write will be linked to the research. However, as I have mentioned before, research into strategies employees can use to address their energy has been very limited, to my surprise I found none that related to coaching or specifically addressed senior employees.

Figure 4.1 illustrates the process an executive coach can follow in order to decide whether, and how, to address this issue with a client. We can now explore each stage in detail.

Assessment

The starting point in deciding whether to address the issue of energy with clients is to actively assess the client's energy levels in a session by reflecting on what we, the coach, witness and by listening for cues in what they say. Sometimes signs may be obvious and other times it may come from being present to the client, really tuning in to their field, to non-verbal clues (Orriss, 2005), the relationship and what is going on

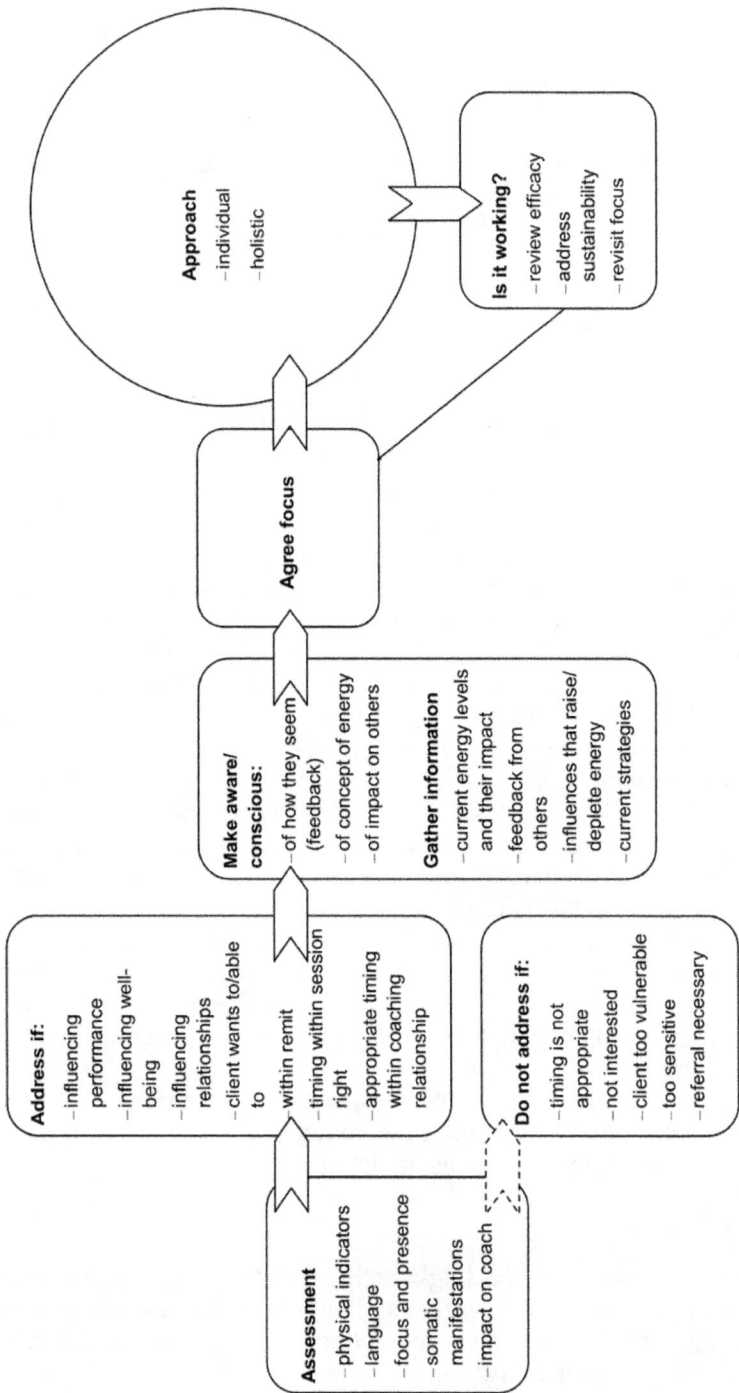

Figure 4.1 Addressing energy in executive coaching: the process

inside the coach. Dan Siegel in his book *Mind* (2017) describes presence as openness and curiosity, empathy, acceptance and deep connection with the client, working to sense the inner life of another. Both Orriss (2005) and Siegel (2017) suggest that when we are present with someone our two energy fields interconnect and we start to exchange information.

This initial identification, assessment and interpretation is subjective, it will be influenced both by the coach's frame of reference and what they are interested in. However, here are some of the basic indicators which can be considered by an executive coach.

Physical indicators: what you see:

- Their body language: how are they showing up?
- Does the client seem physically tense?
- Are there indicators in their facial expression?

What you hear:

- What is their tone of voice?
- What are you picking up regarding their pace of speaking?
- What language are they using which might be indicative of their energy level?
- What do they tell you or hint at regarding their energy?

What you may experience relationally:

- Are they able to focus on what you are talking about?
- Are they really present in the conversation, demonstrating high-quality attention?
- How does their attention, focus and presence sustain during the entirety of the session?
- What impact are they having on you, your energy levels, somatically (the impact on you physically, in your body)?
- What do you notice intuitively with regard to the client's energy levels?

Some clients I find more energising than others. I will be looking forward to seeing them. My energy levels will go up when I'm thinking about meeting that particular person. For other people, my energy levels will be more muted. That's interesting data in itself. [...] And then noticing what happens to my energy as I interact with the client's energy.

Decision making regarding whether to address the client's energy levels

As well as when it has been explicitly requested, coaches can decide to address a client's energy if it seems to be problematic for any number of reasons. For example, it might be that it is influencing the client's performance, well-being and relationships. Some coaches interviewed talked about when they will raise the issue of a client's energy in a session:

> If they look tired. Sometimes you go in and someone's speaking slowly and they just look awful. I would immediately address that.

> If they're not achieving their objectives, I want to try and look with them at what's happening. What's blocking them? And that can be energy, for one reason or another.

> When they come in (to a session) and they're overly bouncy and they're not listening. And I'll say to them, "Whoa, I feel as if a tornado's just come into the room!"

Some coaches may choose to address energy with all clients, even those with optimal energy, in order to make the client aware that this is the case, consider its sustainability and explore whether they are making full use of their energy within their organisation.

> It's such a fundamental part of what makes people tick, and if they're really ticking well, why is that? What's going on?

A number of factors need to be taken into account when deciding whether it is appropriate to raise the issue in coaching, such as whether it is within the coach's remit and if sufficient trust and rapport has been established with the client. There will be a number of barriers to raising the issue of energy in a session, for example:

- Timing within the session, it might be nearing the end of the session and would require more time to raise and explore
- Timing within the coaching relationship, it could be too early on in the relationship, trust may not be established, there may be more pressing issues to focus on or the client may not be ready for such feedback
- A client may not be interested in addressing their energy levels in coaching because they do not see it as relevant, they are focused on other issues or it is not what they want to use their coaching time addressing
- The client could not cope with the issue being raised due to vulnerability, for example, if they thought that it was

unacceptable to raise the subject in their organisation because it is not the sort of place where they can admit to having no energy or feel able to discuss anything that they fear could be interpreted as a weakness

- The issue is related to something too painful or sensitive

I work with one client, and I've worked with him for several years now, and he said at the very beginning, "I have a very bad relationship with my wife. I know that affects my work and my energy. We are not talking about it in our sessions".

If there is any doubt in the coach's mind about the appropriateness of addressing a client's energy this can be taken to supervision. For example, when the client's depleted or inappropriate high energy may be indicative of a need for referral.

Referral

Both depleted and inappropriate high energy may warrant professional assessment if thought to be due to an underlying health condition, as mentioned in Chapters 1 and 2, so it is very important that coaches make an appropriate referral if it becomes apparent that alternative interventions are necessary. In addition, whatever a particular coach's belief is about the boundaries between coaching and counselling or therapy, they need to recognise when coaching may be of little use or is not the most appropriate intervention, for example, for addressing psychological issues such as depression, burnout, problematic anxiety and mania which are 'diagnosable conditions' that coaching is not designed to address. Clients may require counselling or therapy for any number of reasons. It is made clear in the guidelines produced by professional membership organisations such as EMCC or ICF that it is the coach's ethical responsibility to recognise the boundaries of their competence and to encourage the client to self-refer or to refer directly if necessary. The ICF guidelines (Hullinger and DiGirolamo, 2018) specifically mention that referral should be made if the intervention would be important for recovery; the client's daily functioning is being affected or the issue of concern is a barrier to making progress in coaching. All of which are relevant when a client's energy levels are truly problematic. In addition, at any time the client needs advice that a coach is not qualified to offer, for example on nutrition or exercise, working with a relevant, trained practitioner should be suggested.

Coaches will need to know how to identify the need for referral and when, and how, to raise the issue with the client and the vast majority of us will have supervisors with whom we can discuss this and any concerns we have about the boundaries of our practice. If not confident in how to refer, as well as raising it with their supervisor, a coach can consult the relevant guidelines from their professional membership organisation (and then hopefully address identified gaps in knowledge in ongoing training and development activities).

There is a strong case for coaches and coach supervisors to be trained in how to recognise signs of mental health issues so that they know when to refer on and fully understand that it is not a coach's role to offer diagnostic advice to clients (Cavanagh and Buckley, 2014, p. 405). A detailed consideration of this important subject is beyond the scope of this book, however there will be some warning signs that coaches can look out for (Cavanagh and Buckley, 2014; Hullinger and DiGirolamo, 2018):

- When the client is showing signs of depleted energy or inappropriate high energy over a number of sessions
- If there is a dramatic change in behaviour, mood or performance
- If this is accompanied by the client exhibiting repetitive behaviours
- Issues become 'all consuming'
- There is incongruence between what is being said and the client's body language
- Signs of irrationality, delusion or psychopathology, and the client cannot explain why this might be
- The client seems unable to make desired changes
- The client has withdrawn from social relationships and activities
- Changes in weight and appearance, including the neglect of personal hygiene
- The client describes disturbances in sleep (either over-sleeping or difficulty falling or staying asleep)

The coach may not need to stop working with the client when they are being assessed or treated, depending on the condition, as long as coaching and the other intervention are complimentary and the client can still engage with the coaching process. However, there may need to be a pause in coaching or it may be decided that coaching is not the most appropriate intervention and the coach will need to manage the ending of the relationship.

This raises the question of where the coach refers on to. In the context of executive coaching the referral route should already have been agreed with the organisational sponsor who is purchasing the coaching in the initial contracting phase prior to starting work with coaching clients. Also contracting with the coaching client at the start of the coaching relationship should include when referral might be necessary and how this will be raised and managed. Many organisations have

Employee Assistance Programmes or Occupational Health departments and, if not, the coach needs to have planned referral routes 'just in case'. It is also essential to have contracted with both the sponsor and the client as to when the coach would have to break confidentiality, such as if they believe that the client (or another) might come to significant harm, for example, if the client was having a severe manic episode. Again, it is important that coaches are trained in how to approach the subject of referral with clients.

Raising awareness and gathering information

Prior to considering specific interventions for addressing energy it is important to both bring the issue into the client's awareness and gather information about what the client is experiencing in order to enable them to make informed decisions: thus investigating rather than diagnosing from assumptions about what the client is experiencing and needs. The more we can understand what's affecting somebody's energy, the more likely it is that we are going to be able to help them.

Raising awareness

Coaches can raise the client's awareness in a number of ways including giving feedback about how the person is coming across and what the coach is picking up in the session as well as ensuring that useful feedback from others is made available. The client may also benefit from being given further information about energy.

Giving feedback

The coach giving feedback to the client about energy levels is very useful, enabling them to become aware of what the coach is experiencing. Clients may have some awareness about their energy, but as Theory U suggests (Scharmer, 2008), the coach offering their observations, or encouraging the client to become more observant, can lead to more awareness and to knowledge emerging which in turn allows new possibilities or solutions to arise.

> *They might not have taken that next step or level of enquiry about, 'why am I feeling like this'?*

> *A window on to the stuff that you're not seeing: the thing that's hitting them and they're not noticing it.*

The coach giving feedback and asking about what they are seeing and picking up in the moment can lead to interesting conversations with the client. As well as deeply listening to what the client has to say in response, the coach may choose to enquire further, asking why their energy might be like this and how it could be different and the impact it would have.

Feedback may need to be challenging, for example, if the coach thinks that the number of hours the client is working is leading to energy depletion; if the client is behaving in a way that is difficult to cope with; if the client is unsuccessfully disguising or intentionally ignoring their energy levels and if there is a need to point out the incongruity between what they say and how they come across.

> *Some of my clients seem to think that they can disguise their energy levels but in fact they can't. It's my role to point out the incongruity between what they say and how they come across, what they are actually feeling, for example, by saying, "I imagine you're not feeling your best today".*

> *And I might keep banging on about it, continually raising awareness, "Are these the words of somebody with lots of boundless energy for this"?*

There are times when, if the relationship is sufficiently established and trusting, and the coach thinks the client can handle the feedback, the coach might have to be very challenging. Sometimes it will be very useful to discuss this beforehand in supervision and even practice what the right words might be, before having the conversation with the client. Hopefully, at the start of the coaching relationship the coach and client will have contracted for the level of challenge expected. One coach talked about an intervention they made with a client who was upsetting colleagues due to their inappropriate high energy, they said:

> *"I want to tell you [...] Your staff can't catch up. You'll drive them away. I'd find it really difficult to work with you on a day-to-day basis. I couldn't keep up with you. You would exhaust me. I'd be avoiding you in the corridor. I need to hold up the mirror to let you see how another human being, being with you, is experiencing you now. And you may not like what I say, but I'm going to have to say it".*

> *With somebody with very high energy levels I might ask, "How can you tone it down so that you're not exhausting everybody around you"?*

Ask with curiosity about what we pick up

By working with what we sense indirectly from a client in a session and offering this to them, we can give them further insight: this might be done by picking up on cues through our intuition and what we detect somatically. The use of the coach's 'self' has been said to be 'possibly the highest value intervention you can make' (Bluckert, 2008, p. 144).

So if I notice that my energy is dipping or their energy is dipping, I'll say, "Well that's interesting. What's that about?"

I was coaching a team in an organisation that had been through significant amounts of change and their resilience score was virtually on the floor. I said, "Does somebody want to comment? Everything you're telling me is about the next wave of change. I would really like you to tell me what this score says about this team". And it was the first time I think that anybody had been prepared, number one to ask about it, but secondly to listen to them about how tired they all were.

Feedback from others about how the client's energy influences their impact

It is useful to enable clients to become more aware of the impact their energy levels may be having on others and the organisation, both positive and negative. This could be direct feedback from the coach, or their manager if they are invited into one of the initial sessions, or the client could ask their colleagues what they observe. Some may have had 360 or 180 feedback in one form or another as part of the coaching or some other development process which may give the coach and client information about the impact that they are having. This process obviously has to be handled with great care.

Present information about energy

Some clients will benefit from being given information in order to raise their awareness and insight about the concept of 'energy' and how this is a resource for them and also about influences on energy. Figure 1.4 at the end of Chapter 1 and Figure 2.1 at the start of Chapter 2 might be useful for this purpose.

Having a model might be a useful way of helping to jog people's thinking, one that prompts you around some of the factors that might be involved in leading you to lose energy. Because some of the things that happen to us are not obvious to us.

Further exploration and gathering information

If the client chooses to work on their energy further this will need to be agreed and contracted for, at least informally. The next stage would involve gathering information to enable the coach to understand the context and also to further enhance client awareness.

Gathering information: the four main areas

A good starting point is to explore the client's thoughts about their current energy level and their opinion about whether they have appropriate energy to deal with their challenges. This is also useful data to return to for overall evaluation at the end of the coaching process. Lines of enquiry could include:

- Whether they think that they have optimal energy for their current challenges overall, never, some, most or all of the time (specific tasks or events can be dealt with separately). Energy levels can be explored with a number of techniques such as rating using scaling or by use of a metaphor. One of my clients used the metaphor of a pilot light: at the beginning of our work together they said that it was spluttering, a really low flame, and at the end of the contract that it was burning with more strength. Some coaches may use tools such as measuring Heart Rate Variability (HRV) as an indicator of energy if they are appropriately trained to do so
- How they feel when they are optimally energised, fatigued or have inappropriate high energy. What are the signs that they need to address their energy, physically / somatically (in their body, their breathing), behaviourally, cognitively and emotionally? Clients can be encouraged to understand the warnings that their body is sending and treat them as an opportunity for evaluation (White, 2021)
- How engaged are they with their work? Do they feel indifferent?
- Do they feel overextended by their work?
- Does their energy level influence how effective they think they are in their work?
- How engaged do they feel with other aspects of their lives?
- Does their energy level affect their relationships with others?

Secondly, it is very useful to find out whether the client has already had feedback about their energy levels from their line manager, peers, team members, friends and family.

Thirdly, what the client believes both raises and depletes their energy can be explored, including contextual influences such as organisational culture and workload. The purpose being to help the client understand what might be contributing positively and negatively to their energy levels and in some cases enable them to do less or more of these things and, in the case of the latter, habituate them. Keeping and reviewing an energy record, recording levels of energy at different times (again maybe by using tools such as HRV) and noting what the influences were can identify patterns and possible actions, such as doing more activities that lead to thrive emotions in the future. It is also useful to look at cumulative influences. For example, historically they may have been able to sustain optimal energy levels despite having a demanding role with inadequate resources; however, an additional pressure such as having an ill parent may have been the thing that makes them start to wobble and their energy levels to become far from optimal.

There's a role in helping people to understand their fuel tanks and the things that fill them and the things that empty them.

And fourthly, the coach can ask about the strategies the client is currently using to manage their energy and whether they are working. They can also discuss how they might sustain the use of these strategies and what gets in the way at times.

How to address energy

There has been very little peer-reviewed research into what can be done to address energy and the little there is has focused on activities, referred to as 'energy management' strategies, that can be undertaken to maintain or increase energy for employees and manage cognitive or emotional resources. The research has focused on four areas:

- Taking short breaks and strategies to organise one's work
- Physical strategies such as exercising
- Relational or 'prosocial' strategies which look at the influence of positive interactions with others (sometimes labelled 'emotional' strategies) and
- Meaning-making strategies (also called 'spiritual' strategies) including reflecting on the meaning of one's work and meditation

The more I read the research, the more I became frustrated with the superficial and prescriptive methodology which had been used to tackle what seemed to me to be a complex subject.

A personal, holistic approach to addressing energy in executive coaching

A holistic and personal approach

The conclusion of my research was that there isn't a 'one size fits all' approach as previously researched but that working with clients to address their energy levels needs to be considered in a holistic, self-led way, following on from, and building upon, the assessment and information gathering outlined above. This holistic, personal approach (even choosing terminology that works for the client to describe energy and their chosen interventions) acknowledges that humans are complex systems who will have many personal influences on their energy and will need strategies which are individually appropriate: this in turn will make what they do more effective (Fritz, Lam and Spreitzer, 2011). It also allows for people having different starting points and prior experience: some of our clients may be highly sophisticated in how they address their energy whereas others may not have done it at all bar drinking copious amounts of coffee. A holistic approach can be made up of different actions and strategies which the client chooses to do and interventions that the coach makes in sessions. These may be simple actions or involve complex personal work as detailed in the following chapters.

There are a number of additional advantages to this personal approach.

- It can take into account demographic and work characteristics which influence whether or not a person will use the strategies (Kinnunen *et al.*, 2015)
- It addresses the debate regarding whether energy is 'scarce' or 'abundant', or both (Quinn, Spreitzer and Lam, 2012), giving the coach and client flexibility to consider interventions which will encourage rest and replenish energy, be calming, redirect energy, maintain current energy levels or be energising
- Working in this way provides options for how coaches can address inappropriate high energy by offering a range of interventions. For example, by considering underlying emotions, cognitive patterns and considering ways of calming
- A coach can support the use of, and review the efficacy of, chosen interventions (Parker *et al.*, 2017). Research has shown that social support at work has been shown to encourage the daily use of energy management strategies (Kinnunen *et al.*, 2015)
- It allows the client to choose what suits them based on their individual preferences (Schulz, Bloom and Kinnunen, 2017) rather than being prescriptive and making suggestions based on assumption. The quote below, from a very experienced executive coach, illustrates this beautifully:

I got fired from a series of coaching sessions after three sessions with a CEO. This was a woman who was sixty years old. She's been there, seen it, and done it. Done the pioneering and driven massive growth in the organisation. She said, "You know I'm not sixteen anymore, I'm tired". And I was empathising and sympathising with her about that and following what I thought was her line of interest. It was interesting that actually when it came down to it, she wanted me to fight her. She wanted me to be more robust and say, "What do you mean you're like that? You're sixty, not ninety, come on! Get your act together". That's what she wanted. It was not clear from her behaviour and body language. She wanted a kick up the backside!

Agree the focus

Bearing in mind what influences their energy, the client can then decide with the coach what they want to focus on, what they need and want to achieve. For example, they may want to address: energy generally in their working life (which may relate to their overall well-being); prepare for a specific task or event or work out how to act to address fatigue or inappropriate high energy when problematic, in the moment. Their focus will be influenced by whether they want to:

RELEASE ENERGY
RESTORE ENERGY
MAINTAIN THEIR ENERGY LEVELS
CALM DOWN

In the world I work in it's very fast moving, it's frenetic, it's fast, it's aggressive. So what you're usually trying to help people do is calm down.

There are certain times when we're driving toward a crescendo when you've got to put an awful lot in to get over the next hill, which will be followed by a little bit of respite on the way down before the next hill comes: we know that there's a lot of energy that's going to need to go in at that point, like with training athletes, how do they max at that point?

The specifics: interventions, actions and strategies for addressing energy

The specific interventions the coach can make and the actions the client can take to address energy are like ingredients for a recipe that the client and coach will cook up together. The secondary areas of focus (ingredients), represented below in Figure 4.2, are categorised into those which address physical energy and those which will impact energetic activation, emotionally and cognitively: these will be considered in detail in the rest of the book. The client can choose from the possible options in order to put together a plan to address their chosen focus. This diagram can be shared with the client (or some other representation that is more appropriate) to give an overview of options for what they can do in and out of work and what they want to work on with their

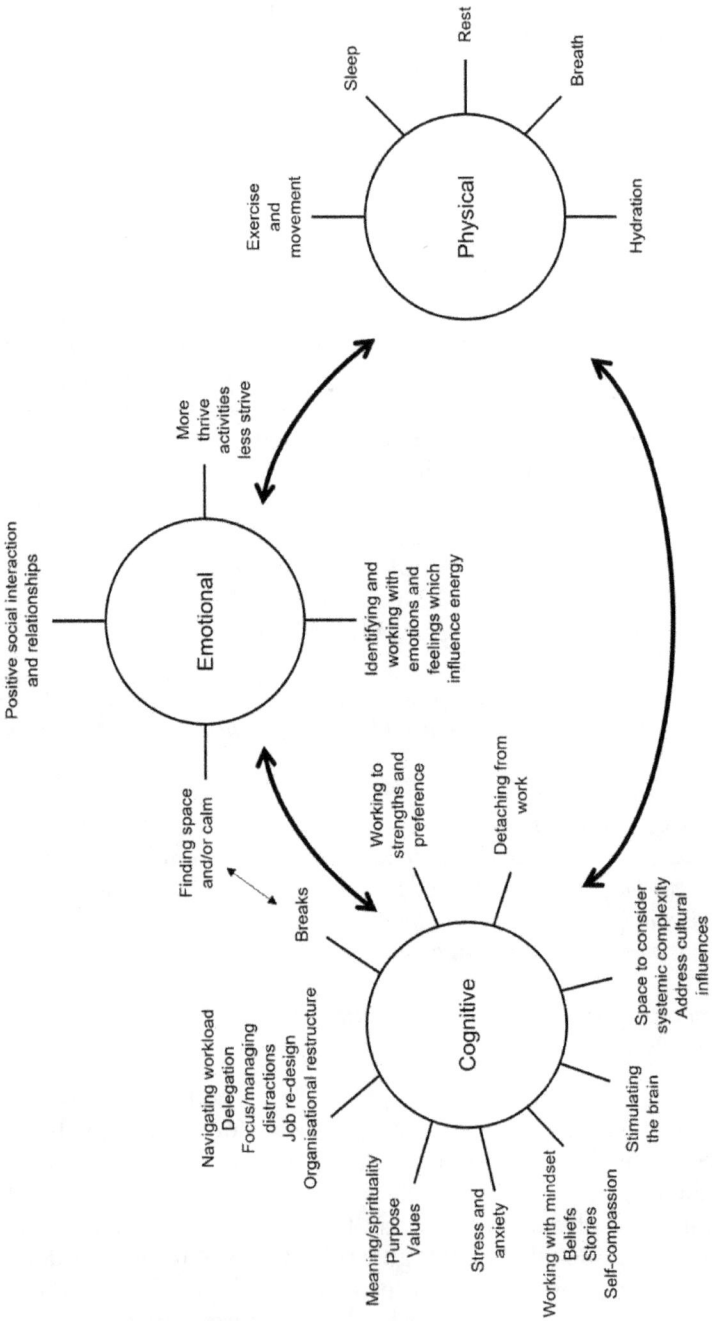

Figure 4.2 The potential areas of focus both in and out of coaching sessions

coach in sessions. As with the ingredients in a cooking recipe these are not stand-alone interventions, they will impact each other.

I was working with a client with a particular focus on their energy. We were unpicking what would have a positive influence and they came up with quite a few ideas. Some were work-related and others were things they could do out of work such as seeing their friends and exercising. We worked with a metaphor, based on the idea that these things could go into 'something' and they could visit this and take out the options when it suited them. The metaphor they chose was a tent in a sunny field which they could visit as and when they needed to.

Small steps

Rather than trying to do too much at first, it is suggested that small steps are taken, actions built into routines and reachable goals set, in order to increase the chance of success. If clients do too much or try to change too much too soon they may fail to stick to the plan and this may feed into the belief that it is impossible to change (writing that for coaches is like teaching grandmothers to suck eggs but someone else might be reading this so bear with me!).

Review and increasing the interventions

It is obviously important to find out whether the client is finding their current strategy useful and whether this is having an impact on their energy levels and their interactions with others. In coaching sessions the coach and client can decide how and when they are going to monitor efficacy, which most likely will involve referring back to the information gathered earlier in the process. One of my clients sends me a review at the end of each week using a scale of one to ten; this is what works for him, being simple and quick, so easy to fit into his busy agenda. He also notes what has depleted his energy and raised his energy which gives us useful data for when we next meet. This reliance on self-reporting does mean that there may be a degree of bias, so some clients may want to gather feedback from chosen, trusted others. If proving useful, habituating the strategies in order to sustain change can be discussed. It is also useful to find out if anything has got in the way of strategies being successful, whether it is resistance to change, a lack of time or some other reason. I suggest that this is carried out before additional interventions are introduced. As the client becomes further aware of their energy and what strategies work for them, additional interventions can be tried. Hopefully they will soon start to do this without their coach.

Becoming regularly aware of energy levels

One of the main aims of this work is to encourage the client to develop conscious awareness of their energy levels in their everyday life and be able to be proactive and take action when necessary. Most people will not have optimal energy all the time: this just isn't possible. But the client, with the help of their coach, can be encouraged to become more aware of their energy at a given time, they may find it useful to scan their energy levels daily (maybe having a reminder such as a diagram or metaphor like a petrol tank) and explicitly consider the early warning signs that their energy needs addressing, taking notice of how they are reacting and thinking.

The personal awareness of energy can be at a number of levels: firstly, energy over a longer time period such as a month or two and the overall impact on their behaviour and performance; secondly, in the moment, such as during an interaction when, for example, they find that they are agitated, wired or tired and thirdly, whether action is needed before a particular event such as a difficult meeting or busy week ahead. Before a specific task or event, the client can ask themselves:

- How they want to show up energetically
- What they need to do beforehand to achieve what they perceive as optimal energy, for example, before a meeting do they need to go for a quick walk, listen to a particular piece of music, take a break and so on
- What are the signals they need to be attuned to in themselves: are these physical, emotional, cognitive or social?
- What might get in the way of them achieving and sustaining optimal energy at this specific time, for example, might the reactions of others affect them? And how might these risks be mitigated? Do they need to prepare to regulate their own emotional and cognitive responses during interactions in order to keep an optimal level of energy and how would they do this?

Some underlying and vital considerations

The relationship with the coach

Coaching for optimal energy needs to take place within a supportive, collaborative, contracted coaching relationship with a skilled, trusted and empathic coach who is as non-judgemental as possible (and aware when this may not be the case). It is important that the client feels able to open up and discuss issues and has the space to reflect with a coach who works in a way that is generative to the client's own thinking. Some of the issues the client needs to discuss in the context of their energy may be difficult, painful and sensitive and in some contexts challenge may be required: all of which needs to be handled with great sensitivity within a working alliance.

Is it pragmatic?

Time limits, location for coaching sessions and contractual boundaries mean that realistic expectations need to be set for what can be tackled in and out of sessions and the amount of change expected. Certain activities may not be pragmatic for the individual, a hectic schedule both in and out of work may mean that they do not, or believe that they don't, have time for certain activities. The location of the session may present limitations, for example, it may not be appropriate for the client to talk about painful feelings and emotions when sitting in a meeting room in the office. Coaching contracts may present boundaries and constraints, the focus for the work may have been agreed with the client and organisational representative with explicit outcomes expected and this may place restrictions on the depth of work that can be undertaken, for example, there may be limited scope for free, non-focused thinking because goals need to be met. However, in my experience, time can usually be found if necessary.

The coach's background and preferences

A coach's background, their beliefs, interest, experience and training will influence their overall way of working and choice of intervention, for example, some coaches will prefer a more structured approach and others to work in a reflective way or work systemically. It will be personal choice as to the extent to which a coach decides to address energy: some may think that working with energy is an essential or fundamental part of their role whilst others will think that it is more peripheral. For example, when discussing addressing physiological influences on client energy one coach I interviewed stated that they didn't find this particular aspect of working with energy interesting and believed that it would not be transformational for the client whereas another thought it was essential. Even if it isn't the coach's priority to address client energy or something that they do very often, having the knowledge about how to do this work is a useful part of a coach's repertoire.

In this book, I signpost categories of intervention and give some ideas for how coaches can work within these and I hope and believe that experienced colleagues will be able to introduce other methodologies into their work with clients which will be highly effective.

The coach's own energy

Executive coaches are affected by influences on our energy as much as our clients and we too need to be very aware of whether we are inappropriately energised in some way and take action. We could be overdoing it, be ill, have been affected by wider events and so on. Relationships are two-way, the client will tune in to how the coach is in sessions and this will include a perception about our energy which they will pick up somatically, from what we say and from whether we seem congruent. So it is very important for the coach to be aware of their own energy levels, that month, that week, in the moment. Do they need to work on this before a session? Has their energy influenced what happened in the session? If working remotely, how do they communicate optimal energy within the session with far fewer indicators available through a screen or telephone? All of this will require awareness, flexibility and understanding. And sometimes energy may be something that needs to be discussed in supervision. It may also mean being careful about how many clients one sees in a day or week: I remember early on in my career coaching three university professors in one day and the Professor of Psychology, the last client of the day, who I was meeting for the first time, saying, "It must be very tiring working with three of us in one day", point made, learning taken on board and I never did it again! In fact it is now very rare for me to see two executive coaching clients in one day.

It can also be important for the coach to consciously consider whether their energy in a session is aligned to the client's or maybe needs to be changed in some way: do they need to adjust how they turn up so that they meet the client's needs?

> I'm very conscious of monitoring myself to both be aligned, but also to step out of alignment so I'm not just responding to their energy but bringing 'an energy' that I think that they need. Sometimes there is a need for the coach to stay calm.

> (Referring to coaching in a specific context) … if you don't go back full on (energetically) they think you're a 'wuss'. You're literally out the door.

Self-compassion

If the client needs to address their energy, the coach can point out that this is not in any way a criticism, it does not mean they are failing in any way; they just need to think about how to keep the metaphorical Formula 1 car performing at its best and also about not crashing into the other cars too much. Self-compassion is considered in more detail in Chapter 7.

Starting a session with a grounding exercise

Some clients may find it useful to start the session with a grounding exercise so that they begin their coaching session feeling maybe slightly more energised if they have come in feeling fatigued, or calmer if entering the session highly energised. Not only can this be energising or calming but such exercises may help to connect the client to the present moment and to reality (Kehinde, 2021). Many coaches will have their own preferred way of doing this. I prefer to design a personalised grounding exercise once I hear what the client would most like to get out of it. This may mean focusing more on emotions, the breath or an area of tension (both physical and emotional). Most of the exercises start with the person having their eyes closed, feet firmly on the ground, sitting up reasonably straight without straining and having a focus on their breathing and then we work from there. It need not take too long. In my experience, some clients like these exercises and others would rather eat their own metaphorical hat. And the location for the session will have influence: working in a hotel foyer might not lend itself to this work.

To sum up

This chapter considers the steps coaches can take to assess whether to address energy with a client and how to start doing so in a session. And how to enable the client to design a way of having a personal, holistic, conscious and proactive approach to managing their energy at a number of levels in the moment when noticing that they have depleted or inappropriate high energy, preparing for events and taking a long term view. Considering what influences their energy the client can decide upon their focus, needs and aims. An overview of the range of interventions a coach can make and actions that client can take has been given and the rest of the book will consider in detail what can be done within a coaching session and by the client outside of coaching to address their energy.

References

Bluckert, P. (2008) *Psychological dimensions of executive coaching*. Maidenhead, UK: Open University Press.

Cavanagh, M. and Buckley, A. (2014) 'Coaching and mental health'. In Cox, E., Bachkirova, T. and Clutterbuck, D. (eds.) *The complete handbook of coaching*, 2nd edn. London: Sage, pp. 405–417.

Fritz, C., Lam, C. and Spreitzer, G. (2011) 'It's the little things that matter: An examination of knowledge workers' energy management', *The Academy of Management Perspectives*, **24**(3), pp. 28–139.

Hullinger, A.M. and DiGirolamo, J.A. (2018) *Referring a client to therapy: A set of guidelines.* Retrieved from International Coaching Federation Website. http://www.coachingfederation.org/client-referral-whitepaper

Kehinde, A. (2021) Ground yourself in times of chaos. In Parsons, A.A., Jackson, S. and Arnold, J. (eds.) *Empowerment in health and wellness.* Hertfordshire: Panoma Press, pp. 35–44.

Kinnunen, U., Feldt, T., de Bloom. J. and Korpela, K. (2015) 'Patterns of daily energy management at work: Relations to employee well-being and job characteristics', *International Archives of Occupational and Environmental Health,* **88**(8), pp. 1077–1086. Available at: https://doi.org/10.1007/s00420-015-1039-9

Orriss, M. (2005). The working alliance. Understanding and working with the energy fields set up in the coaching supervision relationship. *Diploma in Coaching Supervision Handbook,* 2008/9. UK.

Parker, S.L., Zacher, H., de Bloom, J., Verton, T.M. and Lentink, C.R. (2017) 'Daily use of energy management strategies and occupational well-being: The moderating role of job demands', *Frontiers in Psychology,* **8**, pp. 1–12. Available at: https://doi.org/10.3389/fpsyg.2017.01477

Quinn, R.W., Spreitzer, G.M. and Lam, C.F. (2012) 'Building a sustainable model of human energy in organizations: Exploring the critical role of resources', *The Academy of Management Annals,* **6**(1), pp. 337–396.

Scharmer, O. (2008) *Theory U: Leading from the future as it emerges.* San Francisco: Berrett-Koehler Publishers.

Schulz, A.S., Bloom, J. and Kinnunen, U. (2017) 'Workaholism and daily energy management at work: Associations with self-reported health and emotional exhaustion', *Industrial Health,* **55**(3), pp. 252–264.

Siegel, D.J. (2017) *Mind: A journey to the heart of being human.* New York: Norton.

White, A. (2021) 'Possibilities of using our bodies to empower us'. In Parsons, A.A., Jackson, S. and Arnold, J. (eds.) *Empowerment in health and wellness.* Hertfordshire: Panoma Press, pp. 45–52.

5

Addressing physical influences on energy

PHYSIOLOGICAL PROCESSES ARE A FUNDAMENTAL SOURCE of human energy alongside energetic activation. As detailed in Chapter 2 the quality of physical energy and its impact on overall energy levels has been shown to depend on factors such as nutrition, hydration, movement and exercise, sleep, breathing and our age (as summarised in Figure 5.1) and we can consciously make an effort to review how well we are doing in each category and act to make improvements where necessary. Although we cannot stop the clock ticking, acting to address the first six influences may well help to address the last in the list: the impact of aging.

If our clients overlook, and do not manage, these influences on their physical energy this may well impact them in many ways as outlined in previous chapters. However, despite it being common knowledge that we should take the management of our physical sources of energy seriously, do our clients do this enough? Do they do this consciously? And do coaches work with physiological influences on energy and performance? Despite physiology being such an important influence, it is debatable as to how much it is worked with in executive coaching sessions and the wider coaching and consultancy industry. Some coaches I interviewed believed that working with physical influences on a client's energy is very important if not essential, being fundamental to performance, but thought that it was often not addressed and was taken for granted. Even the coaches who spent less or no time on this agreed that it might be a good starting point, believing that it was the safe and basic aspect of energy for clients to consider.

> I think some individuals have pretty unhealthy lifestyles and sometimes just cleaning up your act and treating your body like it is a temple, rather than a bonfire, can have some immediate or relatively immediate effects on energy.

Coaches can, if it has been assessed to be an appropriate focus, encourage clients to begin to develop more awareness of these physical influences on energy and the physiological signals that indicate that they need to take action and identify what they can do. This chapter takes each category in turn. Addressing many other aspects of influence will have physical implications such as taking breaks, calming and meditation and these are considered in subsequent chapters.

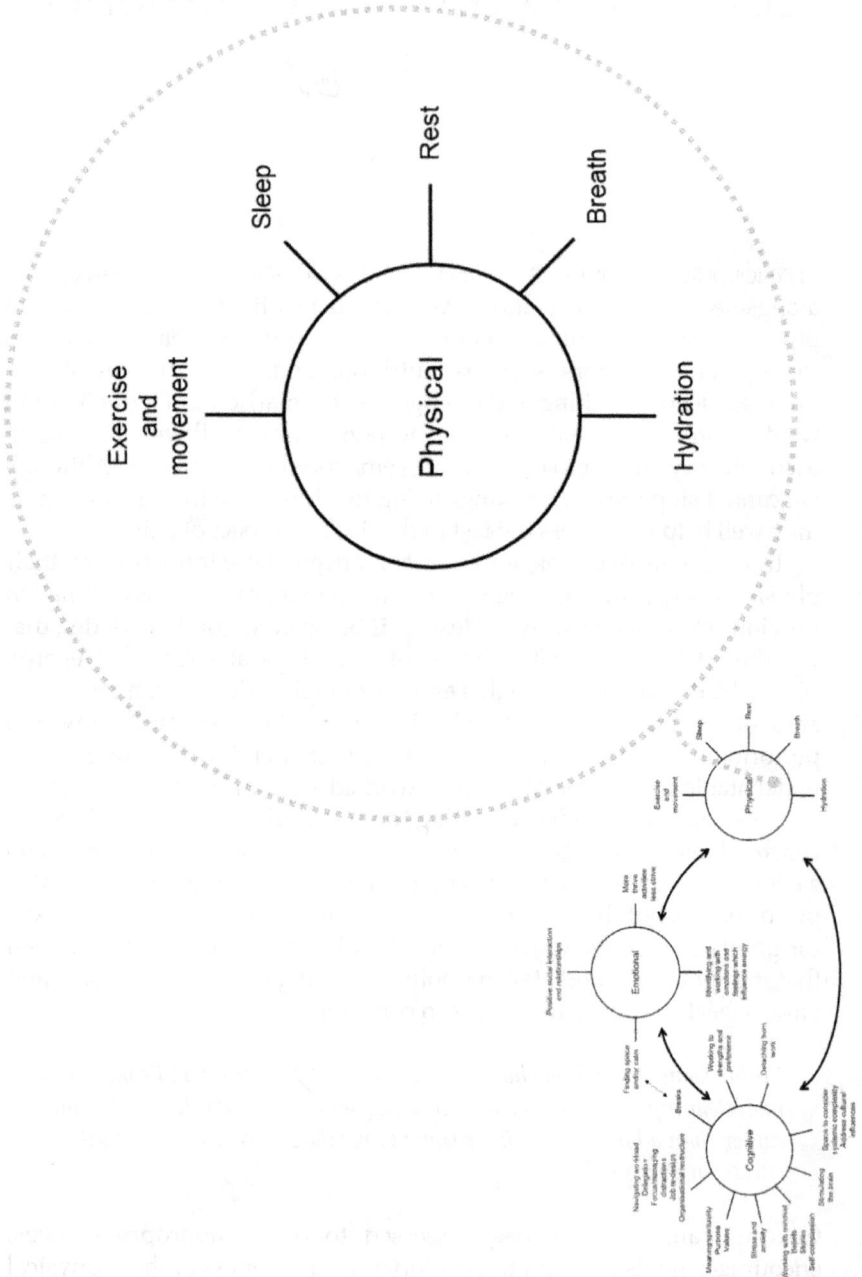

Figure 5.1 Working with physical influences on energy

All the quotes in this chapter are made by fellow executive coaches and reproduced with their permission.

Nutrition

Most coaches including myself are not dieticians, so to reflect how I would behave in my work I will not give any specific nutritional advice (bar an acknowledgement that processed carbohydrates, fizzy drinks, fried food and a diet high in sugar are not good for us), indeed, it is my belief that nutritional planning should be highly personalised. In the UK clients can be referred to the National Health Service (NHS) *Eatwell Guide* (2018) for a simple summary of current advice. But we can work with clients to enable them to develop awareness of the impact that their diet and eating habits have on their energy and help them to plan for necessary change. An initial step might be to keep a diary and use this information to identify what small steps they want to take. It is important to note that the more one makes the decisions regarding one's diet and eating habits in advance, the more likely it is that one will have the willpower to see any aims through.

Clients could be asked:

- Do they notice how some foods influence their mood and energy more than others? How can they eat more of the things that improve their mood and give them energy and less of the things that have the opposite effect?
- How do they feel physically when they have eaten well, eaten the foods that energise them, versus when they have not been eating well?
- What are the central elements of a healthy diet for them? How could they build more of these elements into their routine? Do they need to eat more nutritious meals during the day to stay energised?
- Do they skip meals?
- Do they eat good quality food during the day or grab things on the go?
- What are the most common foods they snack on throughout the day?
- At what time of day are they most likely to have lower willpower and reach for the unhealthy snacks – and what healthy option could be placed in full view instead? Could they add healthier snacks to their routine?

At this point I hesitate to write this, but, as a full believer of the phrase 'a little bit of what you fancy does you good', it is worth mentioning that eating food which you enjoy releases dopamine and the enjoyment of dark chocolate releases endorphins, both of which enhance energetic activation.

Five sessions in, managing in a matrix organisation explored, new job negotiated, my client sat back and looked at me and said, "There is one thing I want to look at. Why am I such a **** in meetings?" We explored what annoyed him, how he felt before he behaved like this, alternative responses and so on. He realised that this behaviour would come on late in the course of a meeting. He started to understand that by this time he would not have eaten and was unlikely to have drunk very much water. We discussed whether both low glucose and dehydration were a factor. So he started to take water and a banana into meetings. He found that it helped greatly, along with a mix of positive motivation and awareness; upping his glucose levels and rehydrating enabled him to have more self-control and feel more positive towards colleagues.

Hydration

Drinking enough water is very important where energy is concerned. Coaches can ask clients if they are drinking enough and whether they think that they could do with drinking more. The current UK NHS guidance is to drink six to eight glasses a day (*Eatwell Guide*, 2018) and other authors recommend two litres (unless intake is restricted due to medical conditions) with the amount depending on physical size, gender and individual requirements (Parry *et al.*, 2017). The fluid should be drunk regularly. This includes water, lower-fat milks, tea and coffee (the latter two, despite being diuretics, are thought to be better than nothing).

Coaches can ask their clients to monitor their fluid intake and notice how they feel physically when they have not drunk enough versus when they are fully hydrated what are their warning signals for dehydration? Clients can also be guided towards apps which encourage water consumption and can be useful to monitor how much water a person is drinking.

Movement and exercise

It is useful to think of movement-related physical health in the context of both how sedentary we are and how much we exercise. It will be useful for the coach to differentiate between the two.

As mentioned before, prolonged sitting affects people's fitness levels regardless of whether they have exercised or not (Kulinski *et al.*, 2014) so it is worth pointing out to clients that, in addition to regular exercise, avoiding sedentary behaviour is important. Clients can be helped to think through how they can make their working day less sedentary. Coaches can enquire about:

- How many times the client does something active during a normal working day and what the activities are
- How they feel when they have been sedentary for too long and, again, what the warning signs are
- What they can do to introduce more movement into their day

Long periods of sitting can be broken up with:

- Low-intensity standing (this could be during telephone calls, between or during meetings)
- Walking intermittently throughout the day, maybe moving around in meetings, taking the stairs rather than the lift. (One of my clients does all her calls and work on a laptop which she has fixed to a walking machine in her home office). Rath (2015) suggests that people can reorganise their work environment so that they have to move around more, for example, have things physically away from their desk so they have to get up

Where exercise is concerned, the client may want to discuss whether they are happy with their exercise routine and, if not, how they would like to both change this and monitor whether they are keeping to their plan in a way that will work for them: for some this might be wearing a pedometer but for others this does not work and sits on their wrist looking like a rather fancy watch. It may be useful to enquire whether the exercise routine that the client has is habit or actually achieving what they need. For example, do they need to build in more exercise which is soothing and calming rather than racing the clock which may potentially make them feel more stressed and feed into the sense of needing to thrash the corporate athlete, as described in the case study below? Do they enjoy their chosen exercise (remember, from Chapter 2, how important enjoyment of exercise is for psychological benefit and sustainability)? What stories are being told to explain why they don't exercise at all or exercise enough and does this need challenging by the coach? And do they do enough exercise in green space?

My client realised that he was very tired having pushed himself incessantly and neglected self-care for a number of years. He was frequently furious with colleagues and very argumentative. It became apparent that he needed to look at what was underlying this highly energised and aggressive behaviour. He acknowledged he was pushing himself on and on but also running on empty. Eventually he was able to look at what self-nourishment meant for him. He designed a package made up primarily of things that he had enjoyed in the past but had stopped doing. He started to exercise more (but also more mindfully so his swimming wasn't always against the clock as it had been recently, so more slow-paced and soothing rather than competitive), eat more healthily and booked himself on a weekend to learn more about an activity that he found both motivating and calming. He also started to play more with his kids. Over the months the value of these activities became more and more apparent. He started to feel more appropriately energised, calmed down and was able to truly work on managing his anger and negative behaviour at work.

Referral to a personal trainer for input into the design of exercise programmes is recommended to put together a programme with the necessary balance between aerobic exercise, anaerobic/resistance and flexibility training and also consider whether the client is exercising enough or over-exercising.

Sleep

Although we know that sleep is vitally important for energy, well-being and cognitive functioning (Kuhnel *et al.*, 2017) I suggest that many people in senior positions don't get enough. There is some disagreement as to how long we should sleep for. A study on elite performance (Ericsson, Krampe and Tesch-Romer, 1993) found that the best performers slept for just over eight and a half hours per night on average (they also took frequent breaks to recharge) whereas most research suggests we need seven to eight hours of good quality sleep. However, Littlehales (2016) challenges the 'myth of eight hours', saying that it is unlikely to be the right amount for everyone. His book and sleep programme looks instead at sleeping in cycles of 90 minutes (and having enough of these cycles over a week) and suggests that we need to begin to understand our circadian rhythms and whether we are an 'AM or PM'er', working out for ourselves how much sleep we need.

Given that the amount of sleep an individual needs differs as do the implications of a lack of sleep on performance, cognition and mood, it is very important that an individual recognises what their own signs of a lack of sleep are. If in coaching we suspect that our client may be lacking in sleep it may be something worth enquiring about. Are their sleep patterns disrupted? What impact is this having on their energy and subsequent performance? What signs do they need to look out for? Can they work towards having a bit more and better-quality sleep? Do they see needing sleep as a sign of weakness? It may also be useful to ask the client how they manage the lack of sleep: such strategies can become the norm and the coach may want to point out when coping strategies may be harmful and have become habit. Coaches can refer them to the literature where necessary. We can also suggest that they see their primary care doctor if regular problems with sleep are raised so that a thorough evaluation of the causes of poor sleep can be done.

Sleeplessness can be due to: anxiety; depression; arthritis; perimenopause and menopause and obviously sleep disorders.

Coaches can help clients think about what steps might work for them. Although many of us have read these tips before I have included a summary for useful reference. For example:

- Turn the bedroom into a sleep sanctuary, purely for rest
- Try to have a cooler bedroom
- Eliminate noises in the bedroom
- Have a blackout blind in the bedroom at night
- Have a bedtime routine for at least an hour before going to bed. For example, practising slow, paced breathing exercises for 20 minutes before going to sleep has been shown to improve quality of sleep, ease difficulty getting to sleep and reduce the number of times and length of time people are awake in the night due to the facilitation of decreased vagal activity (Tsai *et al.*, 2015). Other inclusions into a routine could be to not use electronic devices (the light from which lowers melatonin levels by 20%) for at least one hour before going to bed (yes, we know this, but do we do it?) and dimming the lights throughout the evening
- Jot down one's thoughts for 15 minutes in a journal by your bed before going to sleep
- Go to sleep and wake up at the same time each day (Littlehales, 2016)
- Do not nap for too long during the day
- Be aware of the impact of caffeine, the time you eat and alcohol on your sleep and adjust if necessary
- Don't exercise within three hours of going to bed
- Spend time outdoors during the day, preferably in a natural environment (Shin *et al.*, 2020)
- Consider diary planning to prevent going straight into meetings when getting off a plane particularly when travelling across time zones

In Chapter 2 the concept of sleep debt was considered. This is hard to recover from, for example, it has been shown that eight hours of sleep per day for three days is not enough to recover normal levels of cognitive function (Parker and Parker, 2017). However, Parry *et al.* (2018) suggest that some things can be done to counter sleep debt, such as: 'banking' sleep by increasing the duration of sleep before an expected period of reduced sleep; taking a short rest whenever possible and repaying short-term debt, for example, after long haul work trips or periods of great work intensity by having a few days rest and recuperation (Parry *et al.*, 2018). Long weekend lie-ins labelled 'sleep extensions' can throw the sleep cycle but are recommended in response to short-term or acute rather than chronic sleep debt, whereas taking a nap is recommended as a significant countermeasure to sleep debt in all forms (Leger *et al.*, 2020).

It can take a few weeks to recover from sleep debt that has accumulated over years. Planning a low-key holiday with little on the agenda, and sleeping every night until you awake naturally is suggested, by the end of which the individual will hopefully be getting the amount of sleep that they need to wake up refreshed. Clients can also be asked how they intend to avoid sliding back into a new debt cycle, for example, by building in the amount of sleep they need into their daily schedule as well as following guidance for sleep hygiene.

Rest will be further addressed in Chapter 6 when considering how to find a place of calm.

Breathing

Our breathing patterns alter our energy levels: one of the primary ways that we lose energy is through poor, for example, shallow or erratic, breathing (Watkins, 2014; Nestor, 2020) which can be caused by a large number of factors including anxiety and anger which both typically result in faster and shallower breathing (which can be valuable in responding to an immediate threat). We don't tend to notice these significant changes, however, very quickly such breathing patterns reduce available energy and affect mental and emotional functioning. Addressing this is a significant way of stabilising our physiology (Watkins, 2014).

Bringing awareness to the breath and breathing exercises

Breathing is something we can consciously control, improve and stabilise to improve our energy levels and to calm down: 'willing ourselves to breathe slowly will open up communication along the vagal network and relax us into a parasympathetic state' (Nestor, 2020, p. 15). Years ago, when I started working with my current coaching supervisor I was quite surprised when she asked me, "Are you breathing?" when I was talking about a challenging situation in a session. Her bringing my attention to my breath was powerful, actually at that moment I was breathing in a very shallow way. I learnt from this one intervention and over the years I have become more aware of my breath. What she did for me, in heightening my awareness, is something that we can do for our clients in sessions in order to help them to become more aware, for example, we might ask them to put their hand on their chest to become conscious of their breathing pattern in the moment. We can ask the client to focus on their breathing during the day particularly when they might be anxious or tired and ask them to note whether there are times when their breathing is more shallow or erratic, for example, when multitasking. We can also recommend simple breathing exercises. Simple, mindful breathing exercises to encourage deeper and more regular breathing can be calming and restore energy levels. And, unlike other energy raising strategies people use, like having a caffeine or sugar fix, these exercises don't then lead to a subsequent energy slump. This is likely to be familiar to clients who do yoga or meditate, whereas other clients may find it interesting to consider this from a medical perspective: for example, respiratory exercises used in pulmonary rehabilitation programmes and in cancer treatment have been shown to lead a reduction in fatigue due to better gaseous exchange (Kim and Kim, 2005; Zakerimoghadam *et al.*, 2006).

There are many different breathing exercises, as researched by Nestor (2020), some involving training (and a lot of willpower!). Overall they 'give us the means to stretch our lungs and straighten our bodies, boost blood flow, balance our minds and moods, and excite the electrons in our molecules. To sleep better, run faster, swim deeper, live longer, and evolve further' (Nestor, 2020, p. 202). Some simple messages I took away from his book were:

- Breathing through the nose rather than the mouth allows you to absorb more oxygen
- Moderate exercise improves lung capacity
- Full exhalation and exercises involving slow breathing through the nose, with a big exhale, can lower stress

It is not within the remit of this book to go into a range of exercises in depth; however, I will outline a few simple ones (many of my colleagues will have exercises that they already recommend to clients). Nestor (2020) and Watkins (2014) both offer very informative sections on specific exercises. Where the ones listed below are concerned, ideally these should be done whilst sitting or standing up straight with the shoulders relaxed. (It is important to note that focusing on breathing can be a bad idea for those prone to having panic attacks due to anxiety about their physical state, because focusing on some part of their physiology may amplify the anxiety.)

Simple breathing exercise

Focus on the breath, breathing both in and out. Start to slow it down and imagine the lungs expanding. Breathe deeply for 5 seconds (Nestor suggests 5.5 but I'm not sure how to measure the .5!) into the diaphragm, engaging the lower abdomen so you feel this move outwards, and then breathe out for 5 seconds (5.5!). If this is done six times it will take a minute and if it can be done for longer that is great. Some suggest that this exercise will be more calming if the exhale is slower than the inhale.

The practice can be calming and some authors suggest that it can lead to 'coherence' where the heart, lungs and circulation are working at peak efficiency (Watkins, 2014; Nestor, 2020).

Yogic breathing

Yogic breathing, including alternate nostril breathing, *pranayama*, is conscious breathing practice which aims to regulate energy via breath control. Numerous studies have shown that it can lower blood pressure, heart rate and stress (Pramanik, Pudasaini and Prajapati, 2010; Saoji, Raghavendra and Manjunath, 2019). There are many techniques for doing this but the simple one, *nadi shodana*, involves switching the breath between the left nostril and the right nostril by holding one side closed, breathing in through the open side, pausing briefly, breathing out through the opposite side, breathing in through the latter side and so on.

Heart-focused breathing

Heart-focused breathing is suggested to train the heart to generate a coherent signal instead of a chaotic one, which increases energy levels and improves brain function (Watkins, 2014). Heart-focused breathing doesn't take a lot of time and many people find that it is an excellent way to start and finish their day, but there are times in between when it is especially beneficial, particularly when someone is feeling (di)stressed. This method involves directing your attention to the heart area (maybe by placing your hand over your heart) and breathing a little more deeply than normal. Again, in for about 5 to 6 seconds and out for 5 to 6 seconds (maintaining the ratio consistently). As you breathe in and out, it is suggested that you imagine that you are doing so through your heart, making sure that the breathing is smooth, unforced and comfortable.

References

Ericsson, K.A., Krampe, R.T. and Tesch-Romer, C. (1993) 'The role of deliberate practice in the acquisition of expert performance', *Psychological Review*, **100**(3), pp. 363–406.

Kim, S. and Kim, H. (2005) 'Effects of a relaxation breathing exercise on fatigue in haemopoietic stem cell transplantation patients', *Journal of Clinical Nursing*, **14**(1), pp. 51–55. Available at: https://doi.org/10.1111/j.1365-2702.2004.00938.x

Kuhnel, J., Zacher, H., de Bloom, J. and Bledow, R. (2017) 'Take a break! Benefits of sleep and short breaks for daily work engagement', *European Journal of Work and Organizational Psychology*, **26**(4), pp. 481–491.

Kulinski, J. P., Khera, A., Ayers, C. R., Das, S. R., de Lemos, J. A., Blair, S. N. and Berry, J. D. (2014) 'Association between cardiorespiratory fitness and accelerometer-derived physical activity and sedentary time in the general population', *Mayo Clinic Proceedings*, **89**(8), pp. 1063–1071. Available at: https://doi.org/10.1016/j.mayocp.2014.04.019

Leger, D., Richard, J., Collin, O., Sauvet, F. and Faraut, B. (2020) 'Napping and weekend catch-up sleep do not fully compensate for high rates of sleep debt and short sleep at a population level', *Sleep Medicine*, **74**, pp. 278–288.

Littlehales, N. (2016) *Sleep: The myth of 8 Hours, the power of naps and the new plan to recharge your body and mind*. London: Penguin Life.

Nestor, J. (2020) *Breath: The new science of a lost art*. UK: Penguin Life.

NHS (2018) *The Eatwell Guide*. Available at: https://www.nhs.uk/live-well/eat-well/the-eatwell-guide/

Parker, R.S. and Parker, P. (2017) 'The impact of sleep deprivation in military surgical teams: A systematic review', *BMJ Military Health*, **163**(3), pp. 158–163.

Parry, D., Oeppen, R.S., Gass, H. and Brennan, P.A. (2017) 'Impact of hydration and nutrition on personal performance in the clinical workplace', *British Journal of Oral and Maxillofacial Surgery*, **55**(10), pp. 995–998.

Parry, D., Oeppen, R.S., Gass, H. and Amin, M.S.A. (2018) 'Sleep: Its importance and the effects of deprivation on surgeons and other healthcare professionals', *British Journal of Oral and Maxillofacial Surgery*, **56**(8), pp. 663–666.

Pramanik, T., Pudasaini, B. and Prajapati, R. (2010) 'Immediate effect of a slow pace breathing exercise bhramari pranayama on blood pressure and heart rate', *Nepal Medical College Journal*, **12**(3), pp. 154–157.

Rath, T. (2015) *Are you fully charged? The three keys to energizing your work and life*. US: Missionday.

Saoji, A.A., Raghavendra, B.R. and Manjunath, N.K. (2019) 'Effects of yogic breath regulation: A narrative review of scientific evidence', *Journal of Ayurveda Integrative Medicine*, **10**(1), pp. 50–58. Available at: https://doi.org/10.1016/j.jaim.2017.07.008

Shin, J.C., Parab, K.V., An, R. and Grigsby-Toussaint, D.S. (2020) 'Greenspace exposure and sleep: A systematic review', *Environmental Research*, **182**. Article 109081. Available at: https://doi.org/10.1016/j.envres.2019.109081

Tsai, H.J., Kuo, T.B., Lee, G.S. and Yang, C.C. (2015) 'Efficacy of paced breathing for insomnia: Enhances vagal activity and improves sleep quality', *Psychophysiology*, **52**(3), pp. 388–396. Available at: https://doi.org/10.1111/psyp.12333

Watkins, A. (2014) *Coherence: The secret science of brilliant leadership*. London: Kogan Page.

Zakerimoghadam, M., Marzieh, S., Anoushiravan, K. and Tavasoli, K.H. (2006) 'The effect of breathing exercises on fatigue level of COPD patients', *Hayat*, **12**(3), pp. 17–25.

6
Psychological: Working with emotions in the context of energy

ENERGETIC ACTIVATION IS IMPACTED by emotional and cognitive influences. This chapter focuses on how the impact of emotion on energy can be recognised and addressed, within and out of coaching sessions, if considered to be a significant influence on a client's energy (as summarised in Figure 6.1). The small amount of research into this has largely focused on the energising impact of positive social interactions, which will be considered first, however, many coaches will work in a far more complex way so I will then consider more in-depth ways of working. All the quotes in this chapter are made by fellow executive coaches and reproduced with their permission.

Social interaction

As detailed in Chapter 2, everyday social interactions have been shown to greatly influence human energy levels and are something that humans need. Where the world of work is concerned, strategies to enhance positive interaction have been shown to improve vitality and reduce emotional exhaustion in those with high job demands (Zacher, Brailsford and Parker, 2014; Parker *et al.*, 2017) but not to be a further drain on energy, which might have been expected (Lam, Wan and Roussin, 2016).

The types of interaction found to have a positive impact on energy generally fall into three categories (Dutton, 2003):

- Respectful engagement: being present; really listening and focusing on others rather than giving them half-hearted attention; showing genuine interest; expressing gratitude to a colleague; communicating positive regard; recognition with genuine interest; supportive communication and making requests not demands
- Task enabling: offering to help someone at work; sharing knowledge, mentoring and teaching; advocating in a more political context; encouraging and nurturing others and feeling pride in what others achieve

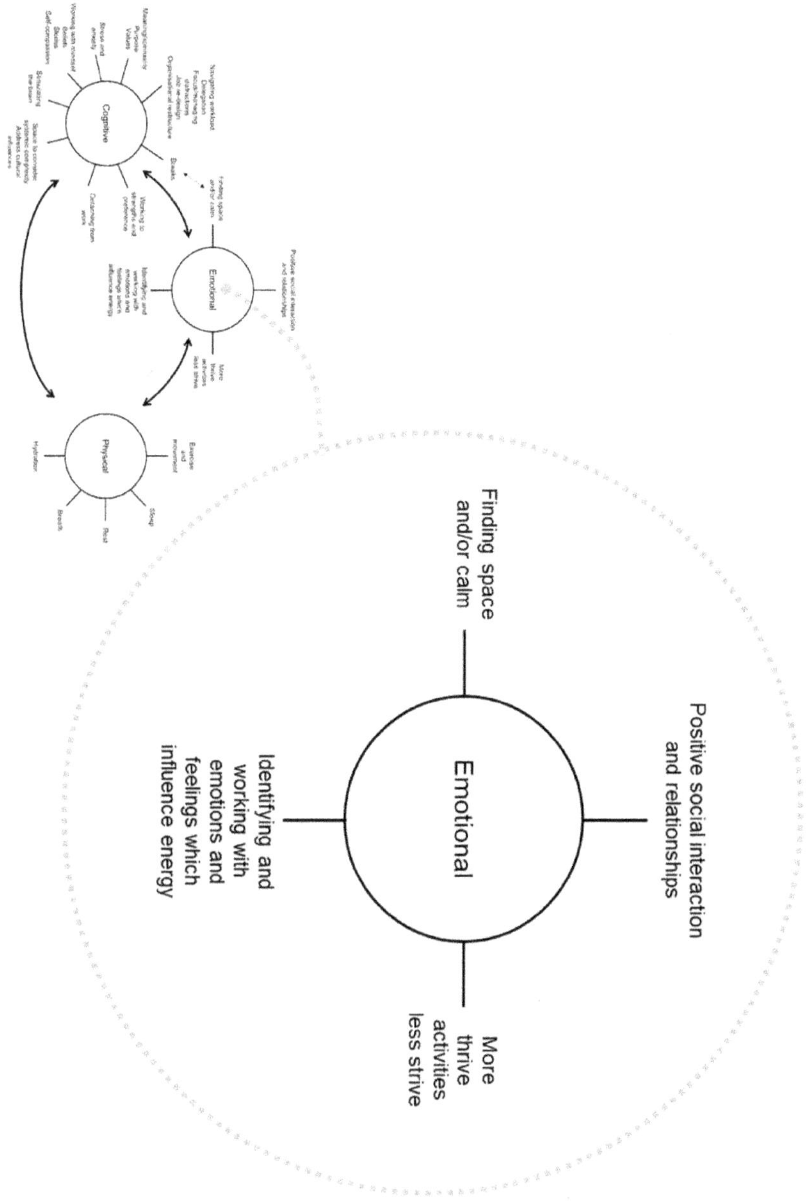

Figure 6.1 Addressing emotional influences on energy

- Building trust: believing people; showing that you have each other's best interests at heart by sharing valuable information; asking for and acting on input from others; inclusive language and behaviour; appropriate self-disclosure; delegating; making sure that people are well resourced and not putting people down

In coaching, the client could explore what social interactions increase their energy, or calm them down. It might be that clients who find interacting with others energising will want to spend a bit more time doing so and also start to initiate this more, rather than mainly responding to others (Rath, 2015). Maybe they can become more aware of how positive interactions are nourishing, replenishing and energising. How this relates to the client's personal preferences can be considered, for example, those with a preference for introversion may find too much social interaction tiring whereas those with a preference for extroversion are more likely to find it energising.

> *I had a very senior client with a massive remit. She talked to me about feeling drained. We explored a number of options for her to address this. She realised that she needed to see more of her sister and actively sought to do this. She said that seeing someone she was so close to more regularly, amongst other things, really helped. It was a little, simple yet powerful step.*

In addition, clients may want to consider how relationships and interactions can be enhanced. For example, by thinking about how further trust could be 'built' with another or within their team or what actions they could take to demonstrate care for others. Are they showing people that they are really listening and interested in what the other is saying? Can they actively work within their team to make it more intentionally supportive and what might that involve?

More and more, interactions are moving online due to home working or being in virtual teams separated by location and maybe time zone. This may present a number of challenges including the lack of opportunity for non-task interaction which would have facilitated emotional connection and bonding (Kniffin *et al.*, 2021). The lack of quality social connection from a 2D screen can be addressed to some extent if the meetings are carried out in a mindful way to ensure that the nervous system gets the information it needs (Porges, 2020). Porges (2020) considers the use of videoconferencing in the context of getting people the social connection that they are wired to need in the context of threat (in this case, the COVID-19 pandemic). He suggests that this can be done in a number of ways which can be considered in advance. These include: welcoming someone into your office via the screen; sharing 'feeling' moments 'not just syntax while video conferencing' (Porges, 2020, p. 137) which enables connection to build at an emotional level; both parties (he stresses that this needs to be bi-directional) working on being as present as possible when talking by maintaining eye contact and using active listening skills (not multitasking and replying to emails at the same time as talking to a colleague). And, lastly, being aware of the importance of shared signals, particularly facial expressions, vocal intonation and gestures which are cues of safety and connection.

But, as explored in Chapter 2, some relationships, in and out of work, can be detrimental to energy, impacting one mentally, emotionally and physically. Obviously this can work both ways, our client may be at the receiving end of difficult behaviour, be instigating the poor relationship maybe by being abrasive or aggressive, or it may be a mutual dynamic. Dutton (2003) suggests ways in which such damaging relationships can be addressed:

- Name the problem and the emotions (see the section on working with emotions in a session, below)
- Identify what can be controlled in order to begin to address aspects of powerlessness
- Address endurance and resilience. This could include: working with possible resultant negative self-image, for example, by discussing the positive feedback they have had from others (some may have an affirmation folder which they can look through, see Chapter 7); spending time with those who are supportive in and out of work and taking breaks
- Work to protect oneself by limiting contact with the person who is having this impact. If this is not possible, consider how much task interdependence can be reduced, maybe by gathering information from others or by building an alternative support network. Psychological strategies such as armouring can be used. I once tentatively suggested to one of my clients, who is particularly down to earth, that they could imagine some sort of armour around them to protect them in a difficult situation. I expected a snort of derision but was surprised when he said, "Oh I already do that, it's a wetsuit. I imagine zipping it up when I walk into the office. But now I am going to imagine having a diving helmet on too": yet another lesson for me about not making assumptions about how clients want to work!
- Address the relationship directly, for example, by using a process of 'respectful negotiation' (Kolb and Williams, 2000)

In addition, a coach can explore why the person the client is finding difficult has this impact, for example, whether this particular relationship mirrors others in their life.

> *My client had a terrible relationship with a colleague who had screamed at them numerous times. He was very affected by their anger. We worked on the impact that this person had on them, why they froze when in their company and also took on a lot of the blame for what was happening. I asked them if the relationship mirrored any other in their life. After much consideration he realised that he responded to this colleague as he had to his older sibling whose behaviour was regularly highly bullying. In the end he reported the colleague's behaviour to senior partners within the organisation and action was taken.*

If none of this works and the situation is very negative, outside intervention may be needed and in severe cases the client may have to leave the organisation.

Enabling clients to understand their impact on others

Clients can be helped to become more aware of the impact that their energy level has on their relationships with others and how this affects their performance, maybe through their own exploration or by receiving feedback. Feedback can be given in a number of ways which most executive coaches will be familiar with: directly by the coach; by peers and others maybe via a 360 interview process (ideally qualitative data gathering by interview and handled in a very sensitive way) or their line manager can be invited into the session to give their feedback in front of the coach.

Some clients may appreciate a more theoretical approach to understanding their impact: introducing theories such as the polyvagal theory (Porges, 2020) and the SCARF Model (Rock, 2008, see below) can be useful to enable clients to understand what their behaviour might trigger in other people. For example, when depleted or inappropriate high energy manifests in their behaviour this may in some way alienate or communicate distance from others. Both theories suggest that the human system is constantly scanning for danger and if we communicate disinterest, unfriendliness or aggression this can send signals of disconnection (when for the vast majority of humans connection is a biological imperative and they need bi-directional interaction to feel safe) and put the other, or others, into a functionally defended state, impacting the nervous system. If their behaviour has such an impact they can consider how to change this with their coach.

One particular intervention to address difficult behaviour, in this case abrasive behaviour, is 'boss whispering' (which the author suggests is also applicable to other difficult behaviours). Crawshaw (2010) bases the method on her theory about how the behaviour develops. She suggests that individuals whose behaviour is frequently experienced as abrasive are 'profoundly lacking in psychological insight into the impact of their behavior on co-worker emotions' (Crawshaw, 2010, p.

62). They do not see their behaviour as unacceptable or unusual because this is their norm (Crawshaw, 2010): they may have grown up in family circumstances which did not lead to emotional understanding so they may lack empathy and be unable to recognise emotion in others as a result. Crawshaw believes that their behaviour at work is based on the fear and anxiety that their professional competence might be damaged. This is driven by a deep need to be seen as competent, with damage to reputation being experienced as a threat to their survival in the organisation which can trigger a fight mechanism, usually aggression.

Boss whispering enables abrasive leaders to address this lack of insight by developing further understanding of their impact and then taking action to address it. Crawshaw suggests that challenging the client's behaviour directly will not work and that the coach needs to really get alongside the client, and once trust is developed move on to helping them monitor and manage this anxiety about damage to competence. The intervention uses an action research method which can be well received by senior executives: data gathering, hypothesis development and testing through experimentation. The starting point is to find out more information about the negative perceptions of the client that in turn threaten their effectiveness, initially via confidential non-attributable qualitative interviews with their colleagues. Further stages involve the client generating research questions and hypotheses, firstly, about which specific behaviours generate the perceptions described in the interview data and, secondly, about how such negative perceptions could be eliminated and prevented from returning thus 'giving the opportunity to gain greater insight into the factors that are jeopardizing continued career survival' (Crawshaw, 2010, p. 65). She mentions that some clients reject the feedback, based on what she suggests is the belief that people should think like them, and that this cannot be challenged, but that presenting information about threat and fight/flight/freeze responses that others may have in reaction to their behaviour, staying with the client's anxiety and reframing the hypotheses can be beneficial.

Do more of the good stuff

An obvious starting point when addressing energy in the context of emotion is for the coach to help the client raise their awareness of their emotions and how they influence their energy and to help them consider and plan for doing more of the activities and interactions that result in 'thrive' emotions and less of those that result in 'survive' emotions. One way might be to stop listening to the news or checking one's phones incessantly for news feeds when it is all getting too much. Some I speak to are now regulating how much they listen to or read the news: they are not out of touch and are still as informed, but they have realised that the resultant (di)stress and sometimes exhilaration was too draining and intrusive to feel calm, preserve energy and regulate emotion, this had to stop.

Finding calm, space and joy

It can be of great use for the coach to explore with the client what they can do to feel calm, content, centred, spacious and joyous (whatever works for them) and in turn generate thrive emotions with the accompanying neurochemistry such as the release of dopamine. This will be very personal. There are many things people can do and most can think of something in the end, although a few might struggle. They might want to do grounding exercises; have time away from their phone; listen to a piece of music; do breathing exercises; paint; view art; read or write poetry and prose; garden; do mindful and relaxing exercise; do yoga; meditate; walk in and observe nature maybe just sitting and looking at the sky or the trees or be with someone with whom they feel really safe and relaxed.

Judy Brown (2008) writes in the first two lines of her poem 'Fire', 'what makes a fire burn is space between the logs'. Doesn't that say it all? Having space in one's day, week, month, life rather than just incessantly piling on the 'logs', the things we take on all the time, will not only help clients feel centred but will give them a chance to rest, recuperate and process what is going on in their life and make connections with others: all of which can restore or create more energy. Simple and obvious, but if it is that simple, why don't we do it? Does the client feel that they need to fill their time, all the time? What might they need to let go of? Do they imagine that if they don't do x, y and z then no one else will and it's all down to them?

> *Fire*
> What makes a fire burn
> is space between the logs,
> a breathing space.
> Too much of a good thing,
> too many logs
> packed in too tight
> can douse the flames
> almost as surely
> as a pail of water would.
>
> So building fires
> requires attention
> to the spaces in between,
> as much as to the wood.
>
> When we are able to build
> open spaces
> in the same way
> we have learned
> to pile on the logs,

then we can come to see how
it is fuel, and absence of the fuel
together, that make fire possible.

We only need to lay a log
lightly from time to time.

A fire
grows
simply because the space is there,
with openings
in which the flame
that knows just how it wants to burn
can find its way.

Judy Brown
Used with permission

The more we get to know our own 'place of centre/space/relaxation'
and what gives us joy, and appreciate the benefits, the better we can
return to this feeling when we are off-kilter, need to recharge our
batteries or calm down. And the more this calming or recharging is
done, the more likely it is that individuals will be able to do it. It might
be that the client can build more of this into their week so that they
develop more of a balance between exertion and renewal. Or maybe
they can begin to recognise when they need to re-centre at a particular
time to regain optimal energy, for example, when experiencing or after
experiencing powerful emotions. A lot of these activities can be tricky
to do during the working day if one is office-based but this could be
addressed by having metaphorically 'bottled up' how it feels when
doing the activity and taking it into work and triggering this, opening
the bottle, when necessary. For example, a client could play the
particular piece of music before going in to make a presentation or sing
along to it loudly in the car when travelling to an important meeting
(this might be more of a challenge on the train!). Some clients may find
it useful to know the documented benefits for some of the activities
listed above. For example, from a neurochemical perspective, activities
like meditation, walking in nature and sitting in the sun release
serotonin, playing with a dog or cat and listening to music releases
oxytocin and watching comedy, endorphins. As mentioned above,
when engaged in such activities people are likely to experience thrive
emotions with all the positive results these bring, including the
restoration of energy (Schaufeli and Bakker, 2004; Fritz, Lam and
Spreitzer, 2011). In addition, research has shown that:

- Meditation and mindfulness can improve the way the brain
  manages its energy (Brown, Kingsley and Paterson, 2015) and

have been shown to increase energy (Aikens *et al.*, 2014), reduce emotional exhaustion (West *et al.*, 2016) and counteract the detrimental effects of stress, survive emotions and sympathetic dominance of the Autonomic Nervous System (Jerath *et al.*, 2015). 'Attention to breath' mindfulness practice is beneficial for emotion regulation with a potential impact on the amygdala and prefrontal activity (Doll *et al.*, 2016)

- Listening to a personalised music playlist (for example, generated by an app) has been shown to: promote relaxation; lower anxiety, stress and accompanying cortisol; lower respiratory rate and blood pressure and facilitate the expression of both emotions and memories (O'Callaghan *et al.*, 2016; Fallek *et al.*, 2020)

- Connecting with nature in a number of ways such as walking or gardening has been shown to have a direct impact on well-being, lessen 'negative' emotions such as anger and sadness (Bowler *et al.*, 2010; Stuart-Smith, 2020), lower cortisol and restore positive mood (Van Den Berg and Custers, 2011). Whilst researching this book I read a post (Bird, 2020) which recommends gardening in a slow and mindful way rather than treating it as a chore and feeling you have to sort the garden out quickly in order to move on to the next task (another log on the fire). They suggest that growing plants from seed is soothing because growth is a process that never changes, is constant and cannot be rushed, in contrast with our ever-shifting thinking patterns

It is important to note that meditation and mindfulness will not suit everyone. Recent research highlights the risks associated with inexperienced coaches introducing such practices into sessions (Bachkirova and Borrington, 2020). For example, for some, meditation and mindfulness can lead to anxiety, depression and stress particularly when practised incorrectly or too intensely. This is one of the reasons why it is important to learn to meditate with a well-trained and aware teacher (Farias *et al.*, 2020). In addition, mindfulness meditation has been shown to exacerbate symptoms of post-traumatic stress.

When enough is enough

With some clients it may be timely to discuss their limits: when will they get to the point where enough is enough? It might be that this challenge has to come directly from the coach. Do they need to take a few days off, or at least consciously replenish their energy, if they realise that they are extremely agitated or exhausted?

Working with emotions and feelings in coaching to address energy

As discussed already, emotions influence energetic activation and can result in optimal, depleted or inappropriate high energy. We may be working with clients who are experiencing emotions that are problematic, which are related to their work (they could be the driver for the client to work incredibly hard), colleagues, organisation or external events. And with those who have learnt to suppress emotion over the years for personal reasons or to conform with organisational or role requirements.

Executive coaching can enable clients to further their awareness of their emotions and feelings, both in the moment and in retrospect. As a result, they can become more able to identify and describe how they experience emotion and more aware of the impact this has on their thinking and behaviour and subsequently their energy levels. They may choose to consider their triggers and responses and address how they would like to work with them. These being stages in the process of 'emotion regulation' (Gross, 1998; Grandey, 2000) which we will explore in more detail below: a knock-on effect of this work being that clients may become better at understanding the emotions, concerns and motivations of others.

Many clients may not be used to talking about their emotions. It is my experience that emotions are not often discussed in the workplace. Also, many adults have grown up learning very little emotional literacy but with top grades in emotional suppression. However, my research partners, the fellow executive coaches quoted throughout this book, spoke about clients quite often becoming tearful in sessions once they knew that it was a safe place to talk openly and got used to being listened to and understood by their coach. How many of us, executive coaches, have worked with a senior client who never truly talks to colleagues about their emotions, doesn't want to 'burden' their partner or friends and then sits in sessions seeming so relieved because at last they can finally talk about emotions and feelings and know that they are being listened to?

I always carry tissues because usually in the second session they cry about something. I've got a bag ready especially with tissues at the front so I can get at them quickly. Usually it's the men: and it's usually the toughest ones.

I worked with a client who was furious with the management of their organisation during a reorganisation. They had to put on the 'front' at work and keep these feelings hidden as much as possible. In the session they had space and time to talk about how angry they were. They talked about it for as long as they needed, I didn't collude, just listened whilst they exhibited total fury as they spoke, for a considerable amount of time, and then left the session seeming exhausted. I remember feeling concerned that they were SO angry. When I next saw them their mood had lifted, their thinking was clearer, it seemed like this release of emotion in a safe environment, where they had felt heard, had had a massive benefit.

I strongly suggest that working with emotions in coaching is not about 'taming' them or replacing survive emotions and feelings with 'better ones' (Waters *et al.*, 2021), nor is it about shaping the client's emotions to fit an organisational context or removing the topic from the coaching dialogue because the coach is unable to work comfortably in this context (Bachkirova and Borrington, 2020). As Bachkirova and Borrington (2020) assert,

negative emotions (to the extent that emotions are either wholly negative or positive) are an intelligent response of the whole organism to difficult situations. ... In all situations, and especially in times of crisis, all kinds of emotions are useful indicators of how the process is going and in coaching we should learn from them rather than set out to tame them or only promote so-called positive varieties. (Bachkirova and Borrington, 2020, p. 24)

When I entered the room he was just furious having had a row with the CEO. He was going to resign there and then. He was in tears, ranting and raving about this person and what had just happened, pacing the room. I let them rant. As they calmed down, eventually they were able to plan what they wanted to do next and script what they wanted to say. They organised a meeting for later that day and by this time were calm enough to go through their key points. They didn't resign and the relationship recovered. We could not have worked on anything other than this in the session nor could any of this process have been rushed.

There are different ways to work in this context, some coaches will be better able, comfortable and trained to work in more depth than others. However, research has indicated that most coaches believe that they cannot ignore emotion and the influence it has on the client in coaching and that it will need to be worked with in some way (Bachkirova and Cox, 2007).

When working with a senior client we did little work with their emotions in the first few sessions. In about session three I immediately experienced him as highly energised, agitated, angry, pacing the room. He had just found out that his new boss was someone he disliked intensely and did not trust. He was in a real state, worrying about how it was going to be, wasn't sleeping: it was exhausting. He needed to process his reactions and decide how he wanted to behave. We worked with the emotion both cognitively and somatically for at least a whole session and revisited the topic over the remaining sessions. It was essential to find space within the remit to do so. In the end, through coaching, he found a way to approach the relationship differently and it worked OK, although it wasn't perfect in any way.

Whatever the method, the work will need to take place within a trusting coaching relationship where the coach is empathic, truly listening and accepting of what is being expressed. The client should never be forced to consider emotions because the coach thinks that it would be good for them and the coach needs to be very sensitive to the client having had enough of the conversation.

Some clients may like to start the session with a grounding exercise that focuses on emotions. As mentioned before, this can be calming, but in addition may bring focus to their emotions which can both raise awareness and allow the intensity to subside. Becoming familiar with how it feels to be grounded can help the client identify the contrasting states when they are off-balance. Others may find 'checking in' useful: discussing how they are feeling at the beginning of the session and considering how this might impact their coaching. Some clients may appreciate this way of working and others really won't, or at least may not be ready to do so.

Emotion regulation

Coaching can enable clients to effectively differentiate their emotions and manage, and respond to, the emotional experiences that they find difficult and those which, in this case, influence their energy. This is sometimes referred to as 'emotion regulation' and the work can involve a number of stages.

Recognition and expression

Firstly, it is useful to enable clients to identify/label, be mindful of and express emotions. This has numerous benefits. For example, it can be a relief for the client because they no longer need to expend energy suppressing the emotion, instead they are able to 'speak', acknowledge and process their emotions. The result can be calming, energising and motivating. It can be such a release to be allowed to really BE emotional. Enabling such awareness in the client can lessen the impact the emotion is having on their thinking and behaviour and being aware of the emotion and related feelings, really aware, can allow the client to be less impulsive when triggered. This goes hand in hand with enabling clients to identify and address how their emotions are affecting their energy. Some clients may find it useful to look at a working model of emotions, such as the one outlined in Chapter 2 which describes the eight basic 'universal' or 'primary' emotions (Brown and Dzendrowskyj, 2018), because it might give them more clarity about what they may want to regulate (Brown, Swart and Meyler, 2009) thus 'being able to name one's emotions, bring them into conscious awareness with a good deal of precision, and regulate them to get maximum value out of them through such a framework' (Lanz and Brown, 2020, p. 34).

Identify what is behind the emotions and the triggers

Following the identification and maybe airing of emotions in the session the exploration may turn to what might be behind these emotions, the triggers (both internal and external) for the emotional reaction, when they are most likely to occur, the accompanying emotions, feelings and thoughts and the related patterns. Where patterns are concerned some coaches, with the appropriate training, may want to look at this in-depth by doing biographical work to identify how these patterns developed (Brown, Hasanie and Campion, 2019; Lanz and Brown, 2020).

It may be useful to discuss how the client perceives threat: whether particular triggers are real and rational, or sometimes the result of over-reaction due to the 'hyper-vigilant, neurotically over-protective amygdala' leading to the perception and anticipation of threat where it doesn't really exist (Watkins, 2014, p. 99). Such an interpretation may be based on past experience: their current response may be because the amygdala has 'remembered' previous situations and outcomes. However, as we know, the threat which the client is detecting may well be very real, as pointed out by Brown, Kingsley and Paterson, 'dangers really do lurk in organisational corridors. But they are the kind of dangers that are best dealt with by clear thinking and calm emotions that have been integrated with thought – with intelligent emotions indeed' (Brown, Kingsley and Paterson, 2015, p. 17).

Some clients will find it useful to take a look at a model regarding triggers to understand why and how they are reacting in certain situations. One such model, the SCARF Model from the field of social neuroscience (Rock, 2008), has identified five categories of social experience (status, certainty, autonomy, relatedness and fairness) which can trigger reward and threat responses, activating the same brain networks as those linked to primal survival needs.

Response and expression

Once emotions are acknowledged and triggers explored, the client may want to look at their responses and how their emotions and feelings are expressed. For example, is their typical reaction to become passive aggressive, maybe avoiding people, or to be abrasive or angry? Or do they experience thrive emotions that allow them to connect, engage and perform? And what are the accompanying physical sensations? Clients may find Figure 6.2 of use to help them understand the impact their emotions have on their energy, thinking and behaviour.

In a coaching session, as mentioned above, being listened to, empathised with and understood can enable the client to regulate. When not in a session, understanding in advance what their triggers are, labelling their emotions and being aware of what the associated impact might be can help the client to both prepare and regulate in the moment. For example, they may be able to reappraise the triggers so that they find the situations less threatening. Labelling and reappraisal together have been found to be more effective at reducing a threat response than emotional suppression (Rock, 2008).

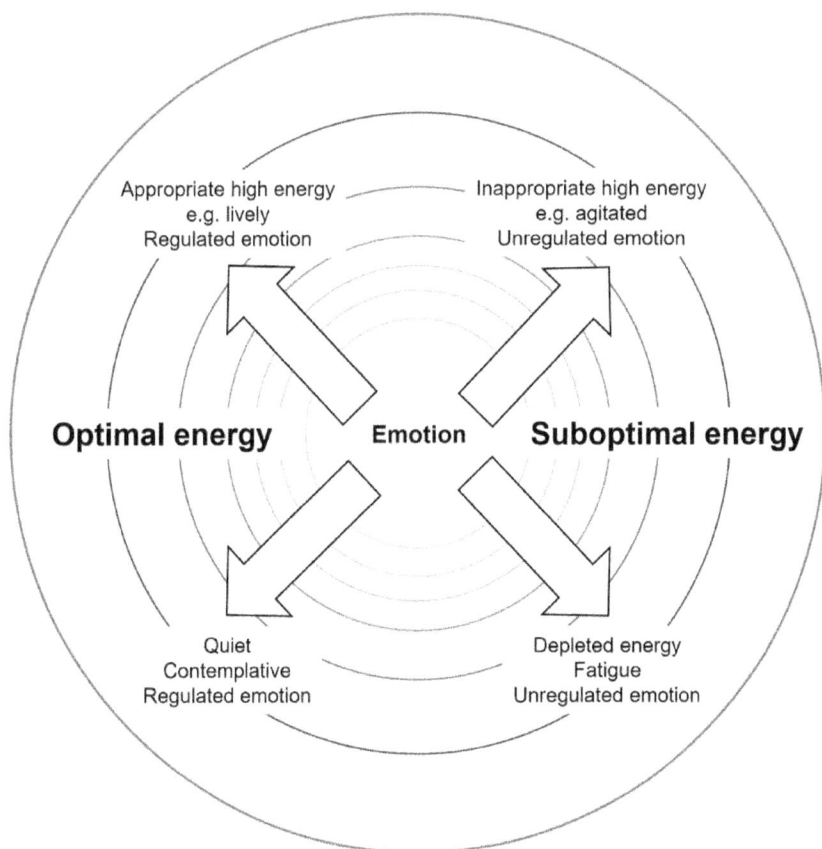

Figure 6.2 How emotion might influence the client's energy

For the management of strong, unhelpful emotions in the moment, as well as naming the emotion, clients can learn in advance how to take deep abdominal breaths, which is a powerful regulator and can lower cortisol levels (see the sections on breathing in Chapters 2 and 5). This might take some time but it is recommended that the person carries on with the breathing until the intensity subsides. It can also be useful to learn to think that the emotion and feelings will pass, and consider what can be done to help this happen, which can include making sure that they don't enter into a thought process that refuels and confirms the feelings and emotions further (Schwartz and Pines, 2020). Kauffman (2020) suggests that it can be useful to be prepared to co-exist with the emotion and suggests that clients can imagine that they are driving a car and that the emotion is in the passenger seat, it is there, but not dictating actions and decisions. It can also be useful for clients to have learnt the skills of self-compassion so that they are not critical of themselves if they experience an emotion. Maybe they could have an internal dialogue which is kinder when they feel the emotion bubbling up again, for example, when they make a mistake, as described in the next chapter. Also, can they become more aware of how they feel in their body when they start to lose the ability to self-regulate and as a result start to take some of these actions?

Working with less conscious or unconscious influences on emotion

In Chapter 2 I looked briefly at the role of the unconscious in influencing emotion and behaviour. Exploring largely unconscious emotions and emotional themes enables clients to access a source of information which can give them a different perspective (Bachkirova, 2011) because it is largely their emotions which motivate and drive their behaviour. This can facilitate transformation, bringing about real, organic change, because reflecting on something previously hidden will move it from 'subject', an unconscious influence, to 'object', something that can be seen and worked with (Kegan, 1994). This is a skilled way of working which can offer useful information to the client, but it needs to be carried out tentatively and wisely.

The role of the coach in working with the unconscious is debated, with some arguing that therapy is more appropriate. For example, Berglas (2002, p. 87) argues that 'when an executive's problems stem from undetected or ignored psychological difficulties, coaching can actually make a bad situation worse' and that therapy is needed to address unconscious conflict. However, I agree with the argument made by Palmer and Whybrow (2008) which is that although it is not the role of the coach to try to make conscious or interpret deeply buried unconscious material, it is appropriate for coaches to work with less conscious influences on behaviour and emotions that they are able to surface easily, and encourage the client to be curious as long as care is taken to manage the risks. Coaches need to be thoroughly trained to work with specific methods and to respect, and not try to break down, the client's psychological defences which are likely to be in place for good reason. It is also essential and ethical that the coach contracts for the use of certain methods with the client and works with 'psychological mindedness' (Bluckert, 2006), considering the impact that their work is having on the client within sessions and discussing this further in supervision.

Two-way collaboration between the conscious and unconscious is helped by the coach creating the right 'space' for the client to think deeply (Bachkirova, 2011), forming a successful 'working alliance' (Orriss, 2005; De Haan, 2008). This can be created by the coach working with deep attention, using gentle questioning and demonstrating genuine empathy to invite clients to tune into their feelings, emotions and thoughts in the moment, without pushing for answers and action. Working in this way allows senior clients, used to working at a rapid pace, to slow down and have space to consider the wider issues without being pushed for a solution (Bachkirova, 2011). Several distinct methods inform this way of working: 'soft thinking' (Claxton 2015) and the 'thinking environment' (Kline, 1999). As a result of these qualities being present in a coaching session, a state of flow may be experienced.

Although some coaches and researchers, such as De Haan (2008), have argued that the thinking environment and relationship alone is enough to provide impetus for change, there are a number of arguments which support the provision of additional interventions. For example, given the short timeframe for executive coaching, working in a purely relational way may be too time-consuming; reliance on cognitive exploration, only working with what is 'conscious', may result in no or only short-term effects (Williams *et al.*, 2002) and some suggest that believing that humans can change their behaviour by thinking alone is both an illusion and biologically inaccurate (Palmer and Crawford, 2013). In addition to the provision of a thinking environment within the coaching relationship there are numerous methods which can be used to work with less conscious influences on emotion, ranging from simple to more complex interventions which can be used to bring information in from the unconscious more quickly, identify blocks to change and also to clarify the desired direction of change. The decision regarding appropriateness of method will be influenced by a number of factors including the subject matter, the individual's ability to deeply explore emotions (Bachkirova, 2011) and their preferences (for example, some clients may not appreciate somatic work, thinking it far too 'new age'). Some methods include:

- Drawing and free-writing methods which originated in psychodynamic theory (Palmer and Whybrow, 2008) that allow the flow of thought from the unconscious without censorship (Ferrucci, 1982) and enable the client to 'sink deeper into the unconscious process' (Holder, 2013, p. 39)
- Pointing out cues, themes and comments that the client has mentioned
- Reflecting back what the coach is experiencing intuitively and emotionally, for example, by saying, "I'm feeling quite sad right now, I wonder if this is how you are feeling?" This type of intervention is based on the idea that the coach's feelings may mirror those of the client's which may not be in their awareness (Palmer and Whybrow, 2008)

I asked a client why they seemed disengaged and sluggish in a session. They said that they hadn't realised that this was the case and started to cry. They said they hated their job and only stayed to keep people happy. On further exploration they realised that this was a learnt pattern from childhood. Surfacing these emotions and their impact on their current situation allowed them to re-engage with the coaching process and to make decisions based on awareness.

There may be an impact on a client's energy due to internal conflict. From an early age humans recognise, and are able to reason about, conflict between different aspects of the self (Starmans, 2017). Such conflict has been described as inevitable 'given the multiple sources of unconscious behavioral impulses occurring in parallel' (Bargh and Morsella, 2008, p. 75). Unconscious conflict can be problematic and tiring, leading to anxiety and block change. The coach can enable the client to become aware of this conflict in a simple way, for example, by asking 'what bit of you thinks that' and whether another 'bit' pulls them in a different direction, and work with the responses to encourage awareness and resolution. Or the coach may use more complex methods if appropriately trained to do so, including an exploration of transpersonal dynamics or diagnostic methods which include questioning assumptions that prevent the client moving forward, such as the 'Immunity to Change' mapping process (Kegan and Lahey, 2009).

Bachkirova (2011) proposes that it is important to work with emotional signals that come from the unconscious via the body, because the language of the unconscious is mostly non-verbal. Much has been written about embodied cognition and the actual processes involved are not agreed upon, however, this does not mean that working with this important source of information should be ignored. It is worth noting that Gendlin, a colleague of Carl Rogers, demonstrated that success in therapy was determined by the client's ability to speak about what is troubling them from the non-conceptual, 'directly felt experience' (Gendlin, 2003; Cornell, 2013). Gendlin developed a therapeutic method, 'focusing', which can be used by trained practitioners to access the unconscious at a deep level, by working with the body to get in touch with, and gather information from its 'felt sense' which is a 'special kind of internal bodily awareness' not recognisable like an emotion (Gendlin, 2003, p. 10). Interventions which can be used in coaching include the coach offering observations about the client's body language, for example, if it does not seem congruent with what they are saying. The coach may choose to work somatically, using the 'whole body to listen' (Shohet, 2008, p. 164) tuning in to, and tentatively mentioning, sensations that the coach is picking up in their body and asking the client if they think that this might mean something. Another intervention that the coach can offer is The Mastery Technique (Watkins, 2014) which uses a combination of breathing exercises and questions to enable clients to convert their inner experience of emotion into an observable, embodied experience.

Working with trauma

I have mentioned before that the experience of trauma can affect client energy in a number of ways including hyper-arousal (when the individual can be highly energised or agitated), hypo-arousal (feeling numb and withdrawing socially) and dissociation (not being in the present moment). Working with someone who is experiencing a reaction to trauma is complex and should be conducted by a skilled and trained coach and only if appropriate, and I stress these last two words. It is essential that referral is made as soon as it is seen to be necessary and the coach does not do anything to make matters worse. The coach needs to make sure that they do all that they can to enable the client to feel safe in the session and slowly learn to down-regulate their defences, explore the cues that they need to feel safe and be able to process traumatic memories. Coaches need to understand how trauma affects the nervous system, the impact that it can have, what the symptoms may be and how to respond. If they don't, they need to refer on.

References

Aikens, K.A., Astin, J., Pelletier, K.R., Levanovich, K., Baase, C.M., Park, Y.Y. and Bodnar, C.M. (2014) 'Mindfulness Goes to Work: Impact of an online workplace intervention', *Journal of Occupational and Environmental Medicine*, **56**(7), pp. 721–731. Available at: https://doi.org/10.1097/JOM.0000000000000209

Bachkirova, T. (2011) *Developmental coaching: Working with the self*. Maidenhead: McGraw-Hill Education.

Bachkirova, T. and Borrington, S. (2020) 'Beautiful ideas that can make us ill: Implications for coaching', *Philosophy of Coaching: An International Journal*, **5**(1), pp. 9–30. Available at: https://doi.org/10.22316/poc/05.1.03

Bachkirova, T. and Cox, E. (2007) 'Coaching with emotion in organisations: Investigation of personal theories', *Leadership and Organization Development Journal*, **28**(7), pp. 600–612.

Bargh, J.A. and Morsella, E. (2008) 'The unconscious mind', *Perspectives on Psychological Science*, **3**(1), pp. 73–79.

Berglas, S. (2002) 'The very real dangers of executive coaching', *Harvard Business Review*, **80**(6) pp. 86–92.

Bird, N. (2020) 'Slowing down to the speed of flowers', *The Floral Project*. Available at: https://thefloralproject.co.uk/blogs/news/slowing-down-to-the-speed-of-flowers

Bluckert, P. (2006) *Psychological dimensions of executive coaching*. Maidenhead: Open University Press.

Bowler, D.E., Buyung-Ali, L.M., Knight, T.M. and Pullin, A.S. (2010) 'A systematic review of evidence for the added benefits to health of exposure to natural environments', *BMC Public Health*, **10**(456), pp. 147–155. Available at: https://doi.org/10.1186/1471-2458-10-456

Brown, J. (2008). *A leader's guide to reflective practice*. Victoria, BC: Trafford Publishing.

Brown, P.T. and Dzendrowskyj, T. (2018) 'Sorting out an emotional muddle', *Developing Leaders*, **29**(Spring), pp. 26–31.

Brown, P., Hasanie, S. and Campion, H. (2019) 'Neuro-behavioural supervision: Applied neuroscience in the context of coaching supervision'. In Birch, J. and Welch, P. (eds.) *Coaching supervision: Advancing practice, changing landscapes*. Abingdon: Routledge, pp. 35–52.

Brown, P., Kingsley J. and Paterson, S. (2015) *The fear-free organization*. London: Kogan Page.

Brown, P.T. and Lanz, K. (2019) 'Coaching leaders with neuroscience'. In Passmore, J., Underhill, B.O. and Goldsmith, M. (eds.) *Mastering executive coaching*. Abingdon: Routledge, pp. 226–240.

Brown, P.T., Swart, T. and Meyler. J. (2009) 'Emotional intelligence and the amygdala: Towards the development of the concept of the limbic leader in executive coaching', *NeuroLeadership Journal*, **2**, pp. 67–77.

Claxton, G.L. (2015) *Intelligence in the flesh: Why your mind needs your body much more than it thinks*. London and New Haven CT: Yale University Press.

Cornell, A.W. (2013) *Focusing in clinical practice: The essence of change*. New York: W.W. Norton and Co.

Crawshaw, L. (2010) 'Coaching abrasive leaders: Using action research to reduce suffering and increase productivity in organisations', *International Journal of Coaching in Organisations*. **29**(8), pp. 60–77.

De Haan, E. (2008) *Relational coaching: Journeys towards mastering one-to-one learning*. Chichester: Wiley.

Doll, A., Hölzel, B.K., Mulej Bratec, S., Boucard, C.C., Xie, X., Wohlschläger, A.M. and Sorg, C. (2016) 'Mindful attention to breath regulates emotions via increased amygdala-prefrontal cortex connectivity', *NeuroImage*, **134**, pp. 305–313. Available at: https://doi.org/10.1016/j.neuroimage.2016.03.041

Dutton, J.E. (2003) *Energise your workplace: How to create and sustain high-quality connections at work.* San Francisco: Wiley.

Fallek, R., Corey, K., Qamar, A., Vernisie, S.N., Hoberman, A., Selwyn, P.A., Fausto, J.A., Marcus, P., Kvetan, V. and Lounsbury, D.W. (2020) 'Soothing the heart with music: A feasibility study of a bedside music therapy intervention for critically ill patients in an urban hospital setting', *Palliative and Supportive Care*, **18**(1), pp. 47–54. Available at: https://doi.org/10.1017/S147895159000294

Farias, M., Maraldi, E., Wallenkampf, K.C. and Lucchetti, G. (2020) 'Adverse events in meditation practices and meditation-based therapies: A systematic review', *Acta Psychiatrica Scandinavica*, **142**(5), pp. 374–393. Available at: https://doi.org/10.1111/acps.13225

Ferrucci, P. (1982) *What we may be: Techniques for psychological and spiritual growth through psychosynthesis.* Los Angeles: J.P. Tarcher.

Fritz, C., Lam, C. and Spreitzer, G. (2011) 'It's the little things that matter: An examination of knowledge workers' energy management', *The Academy of Management Perspectives*, **24**(3), pp. 28–139.

Gendlin, E.T. (2003) *Focusing*, 2nd edn. London: Rider.

Grandey, A.A. (2000) 'Emotion regulation in the workplace: A new way to conceptualize emotional labor', *Journal of Occupational Health Psychology*, **5**(1), pp. 95–110.

Gross, J. (1998) 'The emerging field of emotion regulation: An integrative review', *Review of General Psychology*, **2**(3), pp. 271–299.

Holder, J. (2013) *49 ways to write yourself well.* Brighton: Step Beach Press Ltd.

Jerath, R., Crawford, M.W., Barnes, V.A. and Harden, K. (2015) 'Self-regulation of breathing as a primary treatment for anxiety', *Applied Psychophysiology and Biofeedback*, **40**(2), pp. 107–115. Available at: https://doi.org/10.1007/s10484-015-9279-8

Kauffman, C. (2020) 'Resilience under fire: 5 Pathways to be marathon strong'. 15 April. https://marathon-strong-kauffman-phd-pcc/?trackingId=A

Kegan, R. (1994) *In over our heads: The mental demands of modern life.* Boston, Massachusetts: Harvard Business Press.

Kegan, R. and Lahey, L.L. (2009) *Immunity to change: How to overcome it and unlock the potential in yourself and your organisation.* Boston, Massachusetts: Harvard Business Press.

Kline, N. (1999) *Time to think.* London: Ward Lock.

Kniffin, K.M. *et al.,* (2021) 'COVID-19 and the workplace: Implications, issues, and insights for future research and action', *American Psychologist*, **76**(1), pp. 63–77. Available at: https://doi.org/10.1037/amp0000716

Kolb, D.M. and Williams, J. (2000) *The shadow negotiation.* New York: Simon and Schuster.

Lam, C.F., Wan, W.H. and Roussin, C.J. (2016) 'Going the extra mile and feeling energized: an enrichment perspective of organizational citizenship behaviours', *Journal of Applied Psychology*, **101**(3), 379–391. Available at: https://doi.org/10.1037/apl0000071

Lanz, K. and Brown, P.T. (2020) *All the brains in the business: The engendered brain in the 21st century organisation.* Switzerland: Palgrave Macmillan.

O'Callaghan, C.C., McDermott, F., Reid, P., Michael, N., Hudson, P., Zalcberg, J.R. and Edwards, J. (2016) 'Music's relevance for people affected by cancer: A meta-ethnography and implications for music therapists', *Journal of Music Therapy*, **53**(4), pp. 398–429.

Orriss, M. (2005) 'Coaching presence from the quantum perspective,' *Diploma in Coaching Supervision Handbook.* UK.

Palmer, W. and Crawford, J. (2013) *Leadership embodiment: How the way we sit and stand can change the way we think and speak.* California: Embodiment International.

Palmer, S. and Whybrow, A. (2008) *Handbook of coaching psychology: A guide for practitioners.* Hove: Routledge.

Parker, S.L., Zacher, H., de Bloom, J., Verton, T.M. and Lentink, C.R. (2017) 'Daily use of energy management strategies and occupational well-being: The moderating role of job demands', *Frontiers in Psychology*, **8**, pp. 1–12. Available at: https://doi.org/10.3389/fpsyg.2017.01477

Porges, S.W. (2020) 'The COVID-19 Pandemic is a paradoxical challenge to our nervous system: A Polyvagal perspective', *Clinical Neuropsychiatry*, **17**(2), pp. 135–138.

Rath, T. (2015) *Are you fully charged? The three keys to energizing your work and life.* US: Missionday.

Rock, D. (2008) 'SCARF: A brain-based model for collaborating with and influencing others', *Neuroleadership Journal*, **1**, pp. 1–9.

Schaufeli, W.B. and Bakker, A.B. (2004) 'Job demands, job resources, and their relationship with burnout and engagement: A multi-sample study', *Journal of Organizational Behavior*, **25**(3), pp. 293–315.

Schwartz, T. and Pines, E. (2020) 'Coping with fatigue, fear and panic during a crisis', *Harvard Business Review*, Available at: https://hbr.org/2020/03/coping-with-fatigue-fear-and-panic-during-a-crisis

Shohet, R. (2008) *Passionate supervision.* London: Jessica Kingsley Publishers.

Starmans, C. (2017) 'Children's theories of the self', *Child Development*, **88**(6), pp. 1774–1785.

Stuart-Smith, S. (2020) *The well gardened mind.* London: William Collins.

Van Den Berg, A.E. and Custers, M.H.G. (2011) 'Gardening promotes neuroendocrine and affective restoration from stress', *Journal of Health Psychology*, **16**(1), pp. 3–11. Available at: https://doi.org10.1177/1359105310365577

Waters, L., Algoe, S.B., Dutton, J., Emmons, R., Fredrickson, B.L., Heaphy, E., Moskowitz, J.T., Neff, K., Niemiec, R., Pury, C. and Steger, M. (2021) 'Positive psychology in a pandemic: buffering, bolstering, and building mental health'. *Journal of Positive Psychology*, 17(3), pp. 303–323. Available at: https://doi.org/10.1080/17439760.2021.1871945

Watkins, A. (2014) *Coherence: The secret science of brilliant leadership*. London: Kogan Page.

West, C.P., Dyrbye, L.N., Erwin, P.J. and Shanafelt, T.D. (2016) 'Interventions to prevent and reduce physician burnout: A systematic review and meta-analysis', *The Lancet*, **388**(10057), pp. 2272–2281.

Williams, K., Kiel, F., Doyle, M. and Sinagra, L. (2002) 'Breaking the boundaries: Leveraging the personal in executive coaching,' In Fitzgerald, C. and Berger, J.G. (eds.) *Executive coaching: Practices and perspectives*. California: Davies Black Publishing, pp. 119–133.

Zacher, H., Brailsford, H.A. and Parker, S.L. (2014) 'Micro-breaks matter: A diary study on the effects of energy management strategies on occupational well-being', *Journal of Vocational Behavior*, **85**(3), pp. 287–297.

7

Psychological: Working with cognitive influences on energy

HAVING CONSIDERED WORKING with emotional influences on energy, this chapter will focus on the many different ways that cognitive influences on energy can be addressed (summarised in Figure 7.1). As before, all the quotes in this chapter are made by fellow executive coaches and reproduced with their permission.

Cognition (thinking, reasoning, sensing and remembering) can have a powerful effect on the ability to be energised, enthusiastic and creative. Also, just 'doing' the thinking uses a lot of energy. Research into strategies to address the management of energy in the context of cognitive (usually called mental) influences have in the past largely focused on work-related interventions and I will focus on these strategies at the beginning of this chapter. But, as I mentioned in Chapter 2, cognitive influences on energy can be more complex than this and therefore may need more in-depth interventions in coaching: working at a deeper psychological level with our clients may well be necessary. This can involve helping clients navigate the complexity of their work, their organisation and wider systems and addressing thinking patterns that affect their ability to have optimal energy.

How people do their work: occupational strategies

The limited research into work-related interventions for managing energy has mainly focused on the taking of short breaks and strategies to organise one's work. Obvious additions that can be considered in executive coaching include: enabling clients to ensure that they can appropriately focus on the task in hand, for example, by managing distractions; delegation and working in line with strengths and preferences.

Breaks from work

Most of our clients work very long hours, with little opportunity for recovery during the day, which can affect their energy levels. Taking a break from one's work may not be something clients (or their coaches) think they have time to do and it may be counterintuitive to stop working when one is so busy. But there is a strong case to be made for

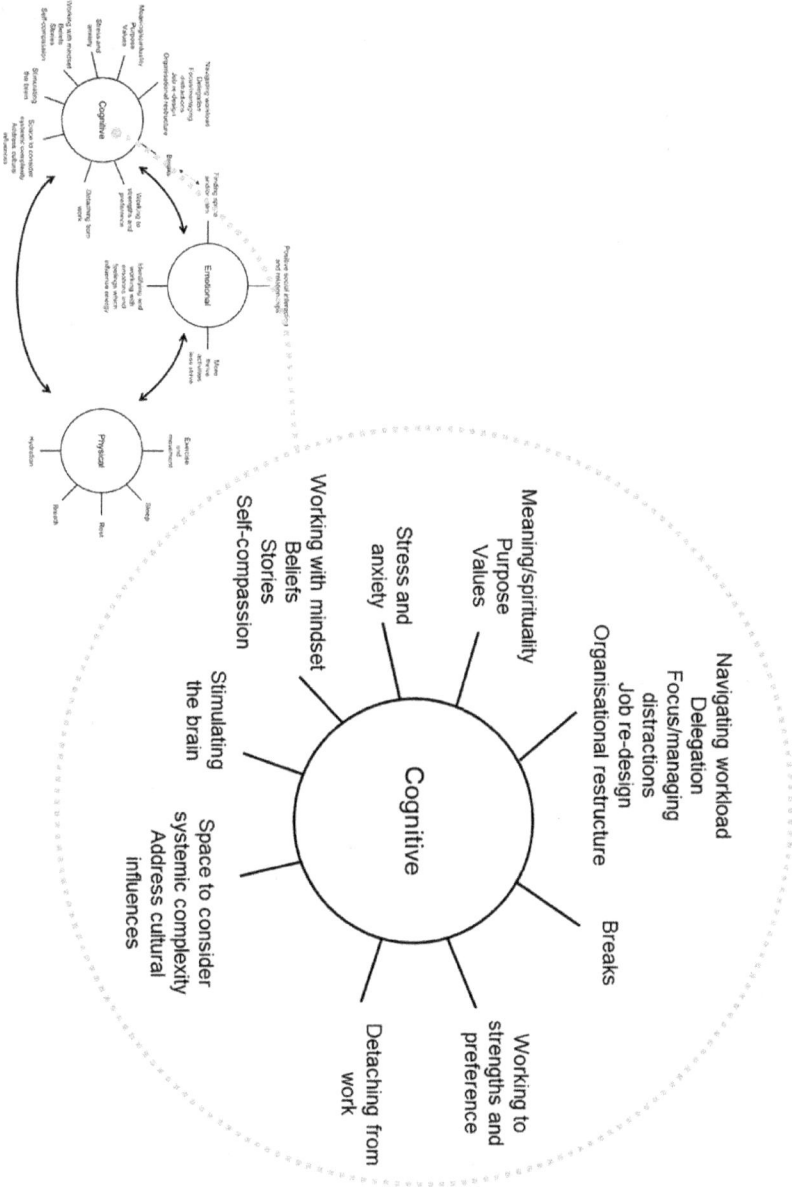

Figure 7.1 Working with cognitive influences on energy

taking a break, even just a short pause when the individual disconnects from work, for example, to have a chat with someone, and various research studies have shown that they have many benefits. Firstly, breaks can prevent further depletion of energy, maintain energy levels, reduce fatigue and make work less taxing (Kinnunen *et al.*, 2015; Parry *et al.*, 2018). Secondly, they lead to an increase in vitality (Zacher, Brailsford and Parker, 2014; Kim, Park and Niu, 2017) and this energy can enable employees to perform their work more efficiently (Fritz, Lam and Spreitzer, 2011; Schulz, Bloom and Kinnunen, 2017) and lead to innovation and creativity (Swart, Chisholm and Brown, 2015).

Thirdly, breaks lead to recovery from overwork and sleep deprivation (Trougakos and Hideg, 2009; Olsen *et al.*, 2016). We need to give the brain a break when we have been thinking for a long time: after a period of work there is a need for rest and recovery. If we don't do this we start to have difficulty concentrating, an inclination to procrastinate and a higher incidence of mistakes. This can be overridden but only by a stress response, the fight or flight response, which floods the body with stress hormones, such as cortisol, that are designed to help us handle emergencies. However, stress hormones that circulate chronically in our bodies may be temporarily energising, but over time they prompt symptoms such as hyperactivity, aggressiveness, impatience, irritability, anger, self-absorption and insensitivity to others (more on this later in this chapter). One recent study by The Microsoft Human Factors Lab (2021) looked at the impact on brainwave activity of being on one virtual call after another in those working at home during the COVID-19 pandemic. It showed that taking a ten-minute break between video calls, in this case using an app for meditation, reduced levels of stress and fatigue. Taking the break allowed the participants to start the next meeting in a more relaxed state, their brains had the chance to 'reset' and the impact on brain activity led to higher engagement in the next meeting.

People at work may now need to be more conscious about taking breaks for the very reason that they are no longer part of normal life in the workplace and also for those working at home it is easy to forget to take time out during the day. Clients may want to discuss building breaks into their daily routine with their coach. One of my clients could only do this with the help of their very strict PA who put the breaks into his diary and no one was allowed to put anything else in those time slots. Or, as suggested by the Microsoft Human Factors Lab (2021) report, is it possible to regularly schedule shorter meetings to allow breaks for all colleagues and for this to become the way that the organisation works?

What to do in a break

Bearing in mind whether the client wants to release energy, restore energy, maintain their energy levels or calm down, the coach and client can discuss what they might want to do in their break. Some, largely research-based, ideas for what to do in a break to address energy include:

- Exercise. (And this doesn't have to be exercise that makes you sweaty and rather unpleasant to be around in the next meeting.) A recent study showed that even a gentle lunchtime stroll of up to 30 minutes can immediately buoy mood and increase ability to handle stress at work. Participants felt more enthusiastic, less tense and generally more relaxed: factors which are very important to productivity and state of mind (Thogersen-Ntoumani *et al.*, 2015)
- Doing voluntary work or having social interactions which are helpful to others (Parker *et al.*, 2017; Fritz, Lam and Spreitzer, 2011)
- Learning something new (Spreitzer *et al.*, 2005)
- Having a short nap. Whilst this may get dismissed by many, brief periods of rest are critical to sustaining energy when working long hours. A power nap has a number of benefits, for example, one study suggests that after a poor night's sleep it can help relieve stress and bolster the immune system by restoring hormones and proteins to normal levels (Faraut *et al.*, 2015)
- Simple breathing exercises to both summon energy and relax deeply. As detailed in Chapter 5, deep, smooth and rhythmic breathing is simultaneously a source of energy, alertness and focus as well as of relaxation, stillness and quiet (Kim and Kim, 2005; Zakerimoghadam *et al.*, 2006) and they also lower cortisol
- Doing an activity which leads to a feeling of real relaxation in the break. For example, a short meditation maybe using an app (Fritz, Lam and Spreitzer, 2011), listening to a favourite piece of music and maybe in a longer lunch break going to a yoga class, a favourite bookshop or gallery (see the section on 'Finding the place of calm' Chapter 6)
- Preferably doing activities that are different from the 'day job': for example, not looking at a screen to avoid digital overload

I worked with a very tired and overwrought COO who realised in coaching that sometimes they needed to leave the office to calm down and recharge. Remembering research on cortisol levels lowering in City of London workers when visiting art galleries for 30 minutes, I asked them where they might go. Not to an art gallery, they said, but to their favourite antique bookshop. They decided that they would go there to 'breathe in' the atmosphere when they really needed to.

Navigating workload

Clients may want to consider both what is specifically sapping their energy work-wise and how they can actively invest their energy in their day-to-day working life. This may lead to simple actions, which even senior clients, in my experience, can still benefit from taking, such as: addressing focus; organising and pacing the working day; deciding what they need to complete, put to one side or pull out of; building in time to think and also more complex considerations which will be considered below. Feeling more in control of their working day can in itself be energy-sustaining (Fritz, Lam and Spreitzer, 2011).

Focus and managing distractions

The human brain functions better when it is highly focused. Having a wandering mind, maybe from multitasking, can drain energy (Killingsworth and Gilbert, 2010) whereas being able to concentrate and be in flow (Nakamura and Csikszentmihalyi, 2009), a state that can be found when immersing yourself into something that you are really absorbed by and find exciting, positively influences energy levels (Schippers and Hogenes, 2011). Yet senior executives are often distracted constantly throughout the day, for example, by emails, phone alerts, social network updates and colleagues. If they can eliminate distractions to some extent this can both reduce the drain on energy and also allow them to spend more time on things that are energising. A client who decides that this is an issue for them may benefit from exploring this further with their coach:

- Do they need to become more aware of when they are, or are not, focusing on a task?
- Is multitasking having an impact?
- What are their main distractions? Might it be their phone? What do they really want to do about this? Maybe they could shut off the alerts at set times when they want to focus?
- Can they identify what tasks they need to focus their energy on during a particular time period and protect the time, for example, by not responding instantly to requests made both remotely and in person?
- What boundaries do they need to set and communicate? For example, identifying specific times to check and respond to emails, or by having different email accounts for home and work and managing others' expectations regarding their response time accordingly

- What do they do that is not a good use of their time, and, can they do less of it?
- Is there a time of day when they are most able to focus?

Considering how one's work is organised and the wider implications

As we have seen in Chapter 3 many demands are made of those working in senior roles (both chronic and acute). How to manage this demand and resultant workload is a useful focus for coaching in the context of energy management. Work-related, or 'organising', strategies such as setting a new goal (Fritz, Lam and Spreitzer, 2011) and checking and upgrading a work schedule (Zacher, Brailsford and Parker, 2014) have been found to lead to sustained vitality. However, Parker *et al.* (2017) found that these strategies may not be as effective in those with high job demands, this may be because setting new goals or having a new 'to do' list highlights that the senior executive already has enough, or too much, work to do. This again underlines why these strategies need to be personal: for some a new goal (including one agreed in coaching) when feeling overloaded might be the last thing they need. It could be more useful to help the client think about what they can really get engaged in and enthused by, and how to get into flow.

> *My client knew that their energy was depleted and realised that if they just had the chance to truly get their teeth into a project, to become truly engrossed, this would really help, as it had done in the past.*

Clients may want to consider whether their workload actually matches their capacity or whether in fact they are overloaded most of the time. It can be useful to look at their priorities in relation to their strategic aims and vision, for example, what they need to do themselves, whether they are sufficiently resourced, what they need to delegate and when they need to say 'no'.

> *I talk to them about dissipating your energy by multi-tasking. I do a quadrant to help them explore 'is it important or is it just urgent?' and assess if they are using their time effectively and explore if it would be better to direct their attention to more strategic work.*

When considering what impacts their energy in the context of workload and resources, the client may conclude that there are wider organisational implications and action needs to be taken. For example, if their remit is just too big, as highlighted in the case studies below, this may even involve the redesign of a role, department or business.

> *I worked with a client who had over time taken on two other senior roles in the business and ended up heading up three functions. This had a*

significant impact on their energy levels. Sometimes they were quite wired, rushing from meeting to meeting, topic to topic, and other times they were very tired. In coaching they realised that this was not sustainable. Something had to go. So we looked at both restructuring and succession planning. Two of the roles ended up going to the current heads of the departments. The client still oversaw these functions but was no longer doing the day-to-day work.

Another coach said, In one session we talked about how he couldn't keep up with all the demands on him and the impact it was having. Right then, in the session he decided to look at how things could be different and used the time and space to scribble down a potential restructure for the organisation. We talked about the pros and cons of various alterations and also how he could argue for change. He gained agreement from the CEO and the restructure happened. He was far more able to focus and perform as a result and felt so much better.

Working more in line with strengths and preferences

The client may also benefit from identifying and working more in line with their personal strengths and preferred way of working. One well-known way of identifying preferences is the Myers Briggs Type Indicator (MBTI) which can also be useful in helping people understand when they are not working in-line with their preferences and that this can be tiring.

A lot of energy gets dissipated because people aren't focusing on their strengths. They're often working in areas of weakness, where they have little passion. And it just becomes hard graft, doesn't it? I think there is a role for coaches in helping individuals play to strength and play to preference, channelling their natural energy towards something they find more rewarding and engaging.

Detaching from work

Research has shown that those who can't detach from work, in that they don't stop thinking about their work, will have further demands made on their 'psychobiological systems' (their neuroendocrine and cardiovascular systems) and internal resources, which can in turn affect their ability to self-regulate (de Bloom, Kinnunen and Korpela, 2015). Also, if an individual is managing their energy at work efficiently they will be more able to detach from work and find it easier to have a relaxing evening and do restorative activities, because they have sufficient resources to do so. Whereas, if they arrive home completely exhausted they may be too tired for the activities that may well have been restorative.

The journey from work to home is a good way to detach from work. However, many more of our clients are now wholly or partially based at home. In the absence of a commute, clients may find it useful to manage the transition between work and home life, for example, by doing a particular activity or having some sort of ritual instead (Kniffin *et al.*, 2021).

Space to address complexity in coaching

As described in Chapter 2 our clients work in complex systems and within cultures that may be negatively impactful on their energy. They may be leading in times of change, both political and organisational, or in crisis situations with or without the appropriate resources. These are obviously topics that can be considered in coaching, with the coach allowing the client to explore their thinking and the related emotions, and strategies for what can be done. They are very likely to relish the space and calm they experience in coaching: to breathe, feel supported and THINK. In addition, the coach may want to enable the client to focus on complex systemic considerations, their place in interrelated and interdependent systems by using specific systemic coaching methods (Whittington, 2020).

Where living with uncertainty is concerned, clients may find it useful to identify what is uncertain in their lives and whether they are upset about changes which have occurred and need to recognise this. The coach could enquire about how they can face the uncertainty, this may include recognising what and who is constant and dependable.

Stimulating the brain: what can be done about 'brain fog'

I wrote about the concept of 'brain fog' in the context of the COVID-19 pandemic in Chapter 2 and it will be relevant to other situations as well as this. In the case of the COVID-19 pandemic, brain fog was identified as a cognitive impact resulting from the contraction of a person's life and the emotional reaction to lockdowns, both of which can impact overall energy, resulting in sluggishness amongst other things. Sarner (2021), having interviewed a number of researchers, recommended addressing brain fog by doing as much as possible to stimulate the brain with new things so that 'distinctiveness' is reintroduced. This could involve learning something new and searching out novel experiences or even just walking whilst on a call or working from a different room in one's house. An additional recommendation was to take part in a variety of social interactions, spending more time with those with whom the individual has healthy relationships. Whatever the cause of brain fog, it is useful to explicitly explore the stress that clients have been under and discuss what small steps they need to take, for example, if they feel that their life has contracted, what they can do to open it up again. It has also been suggested that being in flow could be useful to tackle the state of languishing that many people are experiencing as a result of the COVID-19 pandemic with the accompanying lockdowns (Grant, 2021).

Working with deeper influences on cognition

Clients may find it useful to think about how aspects of their thinking influence their energy. In the rest of this chapter I will consider deeper cognitive processes, looking at: how to work with problematic narratives, address how the client thinks about the meaning and purpose of their work and deals with stressors.

What I present is not a prescription for how to coach but an outline of what might be useful. Some coaches will choose to work in a much more reflective way and barely ask any questions at all, whereas others might find a structured approach useful at times. As stressed before, where deeply ingrained thinking processes are found to be really problematic, for example, where a lack of self-compassion is resulting from difficult childhood experiences, referral for therapy is strongly advised.

Working with mindset

Some clients may find it useful to identify how their mindset, their fixed states of mind and attitudes, might be influencing their energy, for example, by identifying unhelpful common thinking patterns: internal narratives which we may call stories, scripts or beliefs. If considered unhelpful and problematic, for example, leading to self-criticism or lack of self-compassion, it can be very useful for the client to be aware of the narrative and how it influences them. In addition, some coaches may also work with clients to reframe these narratives.

Addressing scripts and limiting beliefs

Humans make sense of their lives and create their reality by constructing and sustaining stories about their 'self' using linguistic functions and imagination to interpret, give meaning, organisation and context to sensory experience (Bachkirova, 2011; Harari, 2015). But these stories may not actually conform to the real world and they can be pretty set in stone, resistant to challenge from others which, if offered, can be perceived as a threat.

Working with clients to address their stories can help them identify the old ones that they run and run. Although these stories may have been real and relevant at the time they were originally formed, this is frequently no longer the case and they often result in the same interpretation of events which in turn leads to the same reaction over and over again. This may cause problems in this context, leading to thought patterns that affect energetic activation in one way or another. In a conversation years ago, Professor Paul Brown talked about a script (with the accompanying emotions) being like a CD: over our lifetime we build up a stack of experiences with stories attached, like a stack of CDs. At times something will trigger a CD, story/ script to play again when it doesn't belong or have relevance to the current time. It can be helpful for clients to realise when a CD from the past is playing and also recognise it's intensity or degree of influence: as one client said to me, "It's not just about it playing, it's about the volume, this one plays very, very loudly".

> *My client started to realise that his remit was just too big. He was overstretched, wired and spending less time at home. We looked at what might be driving his behaviour. He realised that he liked the positive reinforcement that he would get from people saying he was great at what he did. He had a drive to be perfect and hated the thought of failure. This made him stubborn, always thinking that he was right and also unable to turn down the challenge of taking on the extra tasks and projects. He worked on heightening awareness of his thought pattern(s) including the temptation to take on more because he believed it made him look good.*

There are a number of different ways that stories/scripts and beliefs can be addressed with clients, these can involve both identification and rewriting of the narrative. Lines of enquiry can include:

- Whether the client is making conscious choices: what are the underlying stories, scripts, beliefs? Some clients may like to sit down on their own, taking time to think and then write these down. They may find free-writing useful, writing down whatever comes into their head: doing this quickly to give the inner critic less of a chance to pipe up (Holder, 2013). Loehr (2007) suggests that it is useful to write down one's current story by hand (which amongst other things, slows you down and allows you to be more mindful), really focusing on the detail including the thinking behind the story, and to write several drafts until it is an accurate reflection. Then to explore what is faulty about the story and also the feelings that arise. This may take a number of rewrites until the finished article reflects what he calls 'the old story'
- What impact does the story, script, belief have on the client, including their energy? How does it affect them, for example, does it hold them back? Does it affect others? If negative, does this need addressing? For example, the belief that it is important to be liked can have great benefits in the building of

relationships but can make giving feedback difficult, be draining for the individual if they feel that they are not liked, or result in them trying too hard to please others

- Listing the narratives at play. I sometimes keep notes of the ones I hear regularly from a client and, if I think that it will be of use, reflect these back. I also ask them to keep a record of those that they recognise are influencing their energy (and other potential negative consequences)
- What the purpose is behind the narrative: why tell it?
- Do they have narratives which are cumulative or conflicting?
- Exploring the underlying emotions and whether they detect an emotional reaction to the story
- Where might the narrative have come from? Sources may be: the client; another person or a system such as their family, school and past or current workplace culture. The influences may be out of awareness and deeply rooted in the subconscious. If the source is unresolved conflict, both external and internal, or a traumatic experience, this needs to be handled with great care by the coach, if at all, because these may be areas of the client's life that are highly defended and need to stay that way. However, the identification of hidden narratives, where they come from, and the influence they have, can start to lessen their impact. Paying attention to 'the voice' (is it the client's voice or someone else's) behind the narrative can also help identify illogical and destructive thinking (Loehr, 2007)
- Identifying the faulty elements of the story (Loehr, 2007)
- What assumptions influence the story/belief (this may warrant time and deep exploration)? As mentioned in Chapter 2, beliefs are very likely to be based on assumptions (often untrue); an aspect of our cognition that rarely gets challenged. Coaches will have their own way of working with clients to explore these, for example, those trained in the 'Time to think' methodology founded by Nancy Kline will often use the method of deep generative listening and if/when the time is right, ask an incisive question to prompt the client to replace the limiting assumption (Kline, 2020). Identifying the assumption behind the belief can help the client explore whether the assumption is actually fact and, if they realise that it is not, it is likely that it will have less impact: 'to see them for what they are, for the scope of their impact is electrifying' (Kline, 2020, p. 175)
- Consider whether confirmation bias is at play; in other words, is the client paying selective attention to what conforms to their existing belief?
- In addition, clients can be encouraged to be more mindful of when these thoughts come into play again

My client became overwhelmed because they were seen as the go-to person and always had people popping in and interrupting them. They did not believe that they could close their door to colleagues both metaphorically and physically because they thought that they would be seen to be letting people down or would come across as unhelpful and selfish. As a result they had less time for their work and for breaks. We explored the stories, the assumptions and beliefs underlying their behaviour. As a result they recognised that they would not be letting people down. They let their colleagues know that if their door was shut then this was when they needed to concentrate and focus and when the door was open then people were very welcome to pop in. None of their colleagues had a problem with this.

Sometimes there is a need for the coach to challenge the client. I used to have a story that ran and ran: my supervisor had heard it many times, it was really demotivating and energy sapping. In one session with her I started to talk about it again only to hear her say, "I think it is time to stop this story now Viv". My goodness that was a shock (you may remember the potentiator emotions mentioned in Chapter 2, shock and startle, which are thought to lead to change): my wise, calm supervisor telling me to stop repeating this story. Her timing was right, it was well-judged, and it worked. I became far more aware that this was an old story and her intervention helped me to stop running it when it didn't 'fit' the current situation anymore. Going back to Paul Brown's metaphor, the CD was back in the stack, still there, but not playing, and if it tries to play it can be gently put back where it belongs – in the past.

I was coaching a Marketing Director who was passed over for promotion. She was really angry and disillusioned and described herself as being demotivated and disinterested. I took this to supervision. My supervisor suggested that I could ask her what opportunity there might be in the current situation. I wasn't sure that this would work, but in the next session there was a point where this question seemed to 'fit' into the conversation. She really liked this positive way of looking at things and spent some time thinking about this. This, and being able to freely express how she was feeling, helped. She was still angry but it was less dominant and she seemed to be calmer and more centred after the session. She brought up the question of opportunities in the next session and continued to work on this.

After identifying the story or belief, some coaches may work with clients to enable them to re-write or re-frame the story. This process may include asking the client to identify what actions they could take to embed or habituate the new story. Techniques for doing this include:

writing it more than once by hand and revisiting it; speaking it out loud; acting it out and visualising a different 'story', thus re-learning a different sequence of thought and in turn forming new neural pathways.

Addressing the self-critic and self-compassion

We tend to be our worst critics, lack confidence and can be kinder to others than we are to ourselves. We can talk in detail about what we don't like about ourselves but don't appreciate who we are and what we do. This negativity drains energy and limits us in numerous ways and in the long term can be toxic to health.

One way to address the self-critic is to develop the skill of appreciation. Here are three suggestions for how this can be done:

- Explore in coaching what the client values about themselves
- Clients can write down what they appreciate about themselves and look at the list regularly or when most needed (Watkins, 2014)
- They can build up an affirmation folder: a folder of positive quotes, positive feedback and testimonials from others which can be revisited when a mental boost is needed

It can be very powerful to encourage clients to have self-compassion. I have already written about those in senior positions flogging the metaphorical racehorse to the retirement line: it might need to be suggested that maybe they drop the whip and start being a bit more self-nurturing. This involves being able to notice when they are having a difficult time, for example, when things do not go to plan and rather than having a negative internal dialogue and ignoring how they are feeling, instead being kinder to themselves: becoming sensitive to and accepting of what they are thinking and feeling. This can alleviate some of the suffering and worries that self-criticism may produce. Would they speak to their child or their closest friend in the way that they 'speak' to themselves?

It may be that some clients have had to put on a hard-nosed front in their work context, hiding their vulnerability from all, but in my experience, if they trust their coach this front might be allowed to slip away in sessions. This is when they may be able to consider self-compassion, for example, to explore their need to be perfect and hugely critical of themselves as a result. Experiencing compassion in their coaching relationship, with an empathic, non-judgemental coach who is skilled at showing compassion and enabling people to explore their self-critical thinking will help them consider this. The coach can point out patterns they observe and challenge where necessary. As already discussed, the timing for this sort of intervention has to be right. The client can be encouraged to take any number of the following steps by their coach:

- Notice and describe what makes them press the 'self-critique button' and when this is more likely to happen. For example, does it start when the client's workload is very high?
- Become both more mindful of their thought patterns, sometimes called 'self-talk' (this is likely to involve the identification of stories/scripts and beliefs), including the identification of unhelpful 'loops' or connections that can take place in their thinking (Irons, Palmer and Hall, 2018)
- Explore underlying emotions and feelings
- Think about whether sometimes being good enough is alright, and accept that getting things wrong is going to happen, we are all human, it's what we do, and that this is okay
- Work out what the sources of their overall lack of self-compassion might have been. Sometimes this can be a complex process. It can be helpful to understand that there will have been numerous influences, many of which will have been outside of their control and were not their fault
- Consider how they can help to ease their discomfort when they are having a difficult time, for example, how might they calm down (see Chapter 6 and the section on breathing in Chapter 5) and instead react in ways that are helpful and not harmful. Might they need to identify what positive self-talk might work for them? How can they remind themselves that they are on the same side?
- Remember when they have previously been compassionate to others, really wanting to help. What worked, what qualities did they show and what might it be like to experience these qualities for themselves? Also, can they remember times when they experienced compassion or were self-compassionate?
- Write a letter to themselves which is compassionate (from their compassionate 'self' or from a compassionate 'other') about what is really going on with regard to the situation that they are finding difficult, how it came about and how to address it (Irons, Palmer and Hall, 2018)
- Consider what they have recently done well: self-reward in itself may be energising (Kelly *et al.*, 2010)
- Think about what might be getting in the way of self-compassion

The most hard-nosed self-critics, both those who exhaust themselves and those who drive themselves in a completely overly energised way, might like to hear some scientific argument for self-compassion. Self-compassion has been shown to reduce the likelihood of being in a state of threat (due to self-soothing) and to be linked to higher achievement, having a more optimistic outlook and positive mental health (Neff, Hsieh and Dejitterat, 2005; Wasylyshyn and Masterpasqua, 2018). Self-compassion can also enable the individual to have a more compassionate and empathic approach towards others (Neff and Pommier, 2013). This makes a lot of sense, if you drive yourself at all costs, are intensely self-critical and unable to acknowledge how this makes you feel, it will be pretty hard to build positive relationships with colleagues and lead others in a compassionate, understanding and empathic way. Compassion is a core skill for leaders, as Einzig states, having compassion for others bridges 'the gap between cleverness and wisdom – the factor most needed to help us address the multiple entangled issues we face' (Einzig, 2017, p. 54).

However, not all clients will be able to do this work. For example, for some who come from harsh backgrounds, experiencing compassion from their coach and discussing the issue can be very difficult. Other clients may have negative beliefs about self-kindness, seeing it as soft and self-indulgent (Gilbert, 2018). If this is due to heavy psychological defences it might be better to leave well alone in the coaching relationship.

Working with cognitive influences on energy which are not in full consciousness

A lot of what influences both our emotion and cognition will be unconscious or not in full consciousness. Our neural networks are reinforced through repeated use, resulting in habitual, unconscious patterns of thinking (Swart, Chisholm and Brown, 2015). As we have seen in this chapter, habitual patterns of thinking and the resultant behaviours can be problematic when they become irrelevant or unhelpful. When working with cognitive influences on energy which are less than conscious, the coach can enable the client to become aware of these habitual patterns, notice the triggers and when they are active. However, these patterns are hard to change (Swart, Chisholm and Brown, 2015). This requires conscious clarity about the desired change, which can be explored with the coach verbally or by using creative methods like poetry. Once identified, the coach can help the client remember the intention, provide regular feedback and reward small steps in the right direction (Bachkirova, 2011). The desired behaviour needs to be practised to form and strengthen new neural networks (Swart, Chisholm and Brown, 2015), for example, through experiential practice (I have involved an actor in the past). Leadership Embodiment (Palmer and Crawford, 2013) is also a good approach. This method can be delivered by trained coaches to enable clients to recognise the precursor somatic 'marker': the feeling in the body that occurs prior to the thoughts and behaviour that they wish to adapt (Palmer and Crawford, 2013). In order to bypass the set neurological patterns that are triggered automatically, the method teaches the adjusting of the body's physiology and movements to match the thinking and behaviour that the individual wants to introduce.

Our response to stressors and anxiety

Stress covers so many aspects of the person, physical, emotional and mental that it is hard to know where to place this section! As discussed in Chapter 2, we all experience stress and the vast majority of executive coaches will have worked with clients who are suffering the negative effects of stress, (di)stress, with knock-on effects on their work and home life, and causation due to cumulative factors as explored previously. Many coaches will have tried and tested methods for working with clients who are experiencing (di)stress and there are whole books on the subject. A trusting relationship with the coach where the client does not feel further distressed by the fear of being judged or evaluated, and working to enable the understanding of influences, can help. Sometimes the coach will only be able to help the client to just cope with, rather than reduce their reaction to, stressors. And referral might be necessary, for example, if the state of defence is a result of past trauma. The following section sets out the basics: what a coach can do to enable clients to consider their stressors and conscious worries in the context of their energy.

- Some clients who are (di)stressed or anxious may like to start a session with a grounding or breathing exercise that focuses on helpful thoughts including compassion, acceptance or generosity (Arnold, 2021). This can enable the client to feel calmer
- Explore what is causing the (di)stress or worry in the client at the moment: can a list of stressors and cues be made?
- Discuss whether the stress is chronic and/or problematic. The client may be able to rate their stress level (there are stress perception measurements available if deemed useful)
- Explore how the client responds to stressors: emotionally, cognitively and behaviourally. Do they exhibit a fight, flight or freeze response? Are their thinking patterns helpful or unhelpful? How are they judging themselves with regard to their responses? It can be useful to explain the stress reaction maybe by showing a model and outlining the physical, psychological and behavioural components and the impact these can have on energy, both depleted and inappropriate high energy. The SCARF Model (Rock, 2008), as mentioned previously in Chapter 6, can be useful to show how the brain

scans for threat, maybe where none exists. Can a more realistic assessment of threat be made?

- Ask how the client experiences (di)stress somatically, in their body
- Ask how stress affects their energy levels
- Some form of daily self-monitoring or diary might be useful. The client may also find it beneficial to have a notepad by the bed for jotting down thoughts if they wake up worrying
- Look at whether the client experiences vicious cycles including whether their responses to (di)stress have a cumulative effect. Are past stressors having an impact? Using the analogy of building a tower of toy bricks until it wobbles and falls over can be useful to consider cumulative stress: we can build a tower of bricks and it feels pretty strong but if we continue loading more on (in this case both welcome and unwelcome demands) it starts to wobble. Sometimes that one last brick can bring the tower down. It may be that our client was coping pretty well with their large remit, or thought that they were, and then that one extra demand comes along and they start to wobble, the (di)stress becomes palpable and hard to deal with
- When there are multiple causes of their (di)stress it can be useful to explore what little things the client can do right now that might help. Are there work-related changes that can be made?
- Explore what the client can do to recover energetically and physically. What activities might help them to calm the mind (as described in Chapter 6), for example, might a simple grounding exercise or a piece of music help? How might this sense of calm be experienced somatically?
- When the time is right it can be useful to discuss how they can adapt their reaction to stressors and contexts. What is within their power to change? Childre and Rozman (2005) suggest the use of 'reframing', turning (di)stress to eustress, the latter being stress which can enable performance (Kupriyanov and Zhdanov, 2014). For example, a client may want to consider how to manage the (di)stress to enhance productivity, consider why the stressor really matters and whether it can be reframed as a challenge. I suggest that reframing is done only when the coach is absolutely sure that it will be of service to the client, at the right time and tentatively, being aware that a clumsy question might end up with an annoyed client and a rather bruised coach

The more senior clients are, the less likely they are to tell you they're worrying. Let's say they're worried about an acquisition they're going to make or something like that. Or they've got a board meeting. I'll say to them, "Right. I've got a pen and paper, I want you to list now the very, very worst things that could go wrong. What do you dread happening at this meeting? Or regarding this acquisition? What is disastrous"? And I write it out. And I always put it into columns. Then I hand it over to them with a pen and ask them to mark down what is the probability, from 1–10, of these things happening. Then we look at the three worst ones that are most likely to happen and consider the impact. And they'll usually say, "Well actually it wouldn't be that bad after all". I love doing quantification. Most of my clients like working in that way, with numbers.

Learning to decrease and manage problematic anxiety, when the person's reaction is out of proportion to the level of threat, usually involves learning to change some of the ways the individual thinks. But, because anxiety also has a physiological component, biofeedback training from a trained professional, aimed at reducing central nervous system and autonomic nervous system reactivity, can also be helpful (Arroll and Kendrick, 2018).

Working with clients to address purpose, meaning and values: our overall story

As discussed in Chapter 2, if someone finds their work meaningful and it has a clear purpose based on their values, it can be energising and this may be reflected in passion, perseverance and commitment. It is also worth noting that meaning and purpose when accompanied by deep belief and passion can make some people overly energised and oblivious to those around them and their own impact. Senior clients may not have time to think deeply about meaning and purpose, but, if relevant, this can be explored in coaching and a coach can communicate why this might impact their energy levels.

Meaning-making

The meaning-making strategies, sometimes called 'spiritual' strategies, which have been researched in the context of energy management include reflecting on the meaning of one's work and what aspects of it give joy (Schippers and Hogenes, 2011). These strategies have been shown to have a positive effect on energy, for example, reminding us about 'how important our work is, thereby providing the motivation to re-engage with it in a positive way that is energising and not depleting' (Parker *et al.*, 2017, p. 4) and have been linked to raised vitality (Fritz, Lam and Spreitzer, 2011; Niessen, Sonnentag and Sach, 2012). In coaching, clients may want to explore:

- What they personally consider to be meaningful (this may not be related to work or aspiration)
- What meaning they attach to their work. What are they actually doing all this for? Does it make sense for the future?
- If their work lacks meaning why are they still doing it?
- Is there anything left in their work or specific task that could fascinate and engage them again?
- What is pleasurable and fulfilling or would make it more so (Riethof *et al.*, 2019)?
- Meaning relating to events, such as a small exchange. If it is hard to look at the overall meaning for their role, Rath (2015) proposes that they can look at smaller events. He suggests that over time understanding these small aspects of meaning will 'connect the dots between your efforts and a larger process' (Rath, 2015, p. 23)
- The impact that their work has on others, for example, where their strengths and interests meet the needs of others and whether they can take action to make it even more positive or powerful (Fritz, Lam and Spreitzer, 2011)
- Whether the client identifies with their organisation or profession so much that every failure or mistake is traumatic and in turn dents their ability to find work meaningful (Iacovides *et al.*, 2003; Riethof *et al.*, 2019)
- Their 'inspirational vision': can they construct a statement of this vision which incorporates their purpose and is aligned to their values, and then explore the actions that they need to take to address these factors in order to live a more meaningful working life (Spaten and Green, 2019)?

Clients who want to work in-depth on their sense of meaning may be interested in either reading about, or being coached on, the Hero's Journey which is based on the writings of Joseph Campbell (Campbell, 2003; Gilligan and Dilts, 2009). It allows people, over a number of stages or cycles, to work on meaning. Two major influences on development, relationships, work and health are explored: the first being their strengths or gifts which can be used in service of others and the second being the wounds that the person has experienced personally but also in their wider system, family, culture and planet. The overall purpose is to unite different aspects of the self to form a deeper 'generative self'. Clients may also be interested in the work of Karyn Prentice whose book considers how nature and the seasons can be worked with to design the life you want (Prentice, 2019).

As mentioned in Chapter 2, for some, meaning might be spiritual. Connecting to meaning, purpose and values beyond one's self-interest can be highly motivating and energising. Clients may wish to explore spiritual influences on their energy. Sometimes the client may say that the spiritual aspect of their life has been side-lined somewhat and when discussing energy in their coaching sessions they may realise that this needs revisiting. This may mean having more time to practise their faith, finding time for reading spiritual text, regaining connection to their values or through an exploration of their interconnection with the planet and sustainability. Dan Siegel's Wheel of Awareness (Siegel, 2018) is a useful tool to enable people, amongst other things, to explore their connection to other people and nature, as is Neil's Wheel (2020). Meditation and other meditative practices such as yoga and tai chi may allow a sense of connection to a person's spiritual side. However, it can be argued that addressing deeper spiritual influences is not the role of the executive coach and even when the client raises this in a session there might be limits to the depth at which the coach might work.

> We're not here necessarily to solve people's existential problems and they have a purpose which is often defined by the organisation or their role within it. So I think there is a level at which we have the conversation but we probably often don't get to a deeply philosophical or existential kind of level of conversation with people, because it's not what we've been contracted for.

Purpose

It is argued that having a positive personal or shared purpose has a powerful and lasting influence on energy. Senior clients may derive a sense of purpose from their overall role or different elements of it, such as mentoring others, being part of a cohesive team, forming a commitment to treating others with respect and care, or from communicating positive energy (Loehr and Schwartz, 2003). Coaches can work with clients to help them explore their purpose in work or in life overall, a process which requires time, deep thinking and probably a few attempts. Lines of exploration can include:

- What does the client do from day to day that is aligned with their purpose? Is this motivating, inspiring and energising?
- The purpose of their role and that of their team or organisation. Is there any misalignment?
- Is working in line with their purpose sustainable? Do things get in the way?
- Whether they need to do something else that is really important to them
- Whether their purpose is based on needs driven by survival emotions, such as fear, leading to a need to keep safe (as mentioned in Chapter 6, it is suggested that abrasive leaders

have a deep need to be seen as competent which is driven by fear of failure)

- What their epitaph might say. What would they like it to say?

Your energy is there to serve a purpose. The question for me is what's the purpose? If the purpose is the right purpose it will release more energy. One of the very important roles we have as a coach is to help people to explore that.

Values

Our meaning and purpose 'live' in the context of our values. Coaching can give the client the chance to explore and identify their values and, as described by Einzig, make more explicit their 'choice to act according to a clear and personally integrated understanding of what is good, what is right, what serves the whole best' (Einzig, 2017, p. 49). Coaches will have their own ways of exploring values with their clients; they may have a list of values, or value cards, to prompt thinking and exercises that they offer. Here are some areas for enquiry:

- Can they identify their core values? Where do these stem from?
- How much influence do their values have on how they live their life, and how is this reflected in their behaviour and actions, including how they come across to others?
- How does it feel to work (or be living) in connection with their values, or not? How does this impact their energy?
- Are there areas of their life where their behaviour and actions could be more connected to their values? Is there a value they hold that they do not feel that they are acting upon at the moment? What is this and what might they be able to do about it?
- Does the purpose of their role, team and wider organisation align with these values? Has this changed? Is this important?
- How might their values help them cope in difficult, even crisis, situations? The client may find it useful to think about how their values help them to find their way in a hectic world (Loehr and Schwartz, 2003; Einzig, 2017)

It is of value to enable clients to get to a place where they're best suited to the environment in which they're in. In that they work in as near as possible alignment to their values, their beliefs, where they feel they're making a difference, because actually where that happens that releases the most energy.

Looking at meaning, purpose and values in coaching can be sensitive so it is very important that the client wants to explore this, in this case in the context of their energy, and the coaching needs to be conducted with care (Spaten and Green, 2019). Questioning from a well-meaning and enthusiastic coach, who thinks that this is the answer to energy, may backfire if the client realises that their work has little meaning and purpose and that they feel unable to do anything about it. In addition, as mentioned in Chapter 2, research has found that having a meaningful life and work can increase stress, anxiety and exhaustion. So although having no clear meaning or purpose can lead to low energetic activation and poor motivation it doesn't necessarily follow that having meaning and purpose is the panacea for energy. Encouraging clients to consider small aspects of this, if at all, might be all that they need. This highlights the point that what is considered in coaching has to be what works for the individual client, rather than be based on the coach's assumptions or agenda, however well-meaning it might be.

References

Arnold, J. (2021) 'Presence and mindfulness'. In Parsons, A.A., Jackson, S. and Arnold, J. (eds.) *Empowerment in health and wellness*. Hertfordshire: Panoma Press, pp. 13–22.

Arroll, B. and Kendrick, T. (2018) 'Anxiety'. In Gask, L., Kendrick, T., Peveler, R. and Chew-Graham, C.A. (eds.) *Primary care mental health*. Cambridge: Cambridge University Press, pp. 125–135.

Bachkirova, T. (2011) *Developmental coaching. Working with the self*. Maidenhead: McGraw-Hill Education.

Campbell, J. (2003) *The hero's journey: Joseph Campbell on his life and work*. California: New World Library.

Childre, D. and Rozman, D. (2005) *Transforming stress: The HeartMath solution for relieving worry, fatigue and tension*. Oakland: New Harbinger Publications.

de Bloom, J., Kinnunen, U. and Korpela, K. (2015) 'Recovery processes during and after work: Associations with health, work engagement and job performance', *Journal of Occupational and Environmental Medicine*, **57**(7), pp. 732–742.

Einzig, H. (2017) *The future of coaching: Vision, leadership and responsibility in a transforming world*. Abingdon: Routledge.

Faraut, B., Nakib, S., Drogou, C., Elbaz, M., Sauvet, J., De Bandt, J. and Leger, D. (2015) 'Napping reverses the salivary interleukin-6 and urinary norepinephrine changes induced by sleep restriction', *The Journal of Clinical Endocrinology and Metabolism*, **100**(3), pp. 416–426.

Fritz, C., Lam, C. and Spreitzer, G. (2011) 'It's the little things that matter: An examination of knowledge workers' energy management', *The Academy of Management Perspectives*, **24**(3), pp. 28–139.

Gilbert, P. (2018) 'Introducing compassion-focused therapy', *Advances in Psychiatric Treatment*, **15**(3), pp. 199–208. Available at: https://doi.org/10.1192/apt.bp.107.005264

Gilligan, S. and Dilts, R. (2009) *The hero's journey: A voyage of self-discovery.* Carmarthen: Crown House Publishing Ltd.

Grant, A. (2021) 'There's a name for the blah you're feeling: It's called languishing', *New York Times*, 19 April. Available at: https://www.nytimes.com/2021/04/19/well/mind/covid-mental-health-languishing.html

Harari, Y.N. (2015) *Homo deus.* London: Penguin Random House.

Holder, J. (2013) *49 ways to write yourself well: The science and wisdom on writing and journaling.* Brighton: Step Beach Press Ltd.

Iacovides, A., Fountoulakis, K.N., St. Kaprinis and Kaprinis, G. (2003) 'The relationship between job stress, burnout and clinical depression', *Journal of Affective Disorders*, **75**(3), pp. 209–221.

Irons, C., Palmer, S. and Hall, L. (2018) 'Compassion focused coaching'. In Palmer, S. and Whybrow, A. (eds.) *Handbook of coaching psychology: A guide for practitioners*, 2nd edn. Sussex: Routledge.

Kelly, A.C., Zuroff, D.C., Foa, C.L. and Gilbert, P. (2010) 'Who benefits from training in self-compassionate self-regulation? A study of smoking reduction', *Journal of Social and Clinical Psychology*, **29**(7), pp. 727–755.

Killingsworth, M.A. and Gilbert, D.T. (2010) 'A wandering mind is an unhappy mind', *Science*, **330**(6006), pp. 932.

Kim, S. and Kim, H. (2005) 'Effects of a relaxation breathing exercise on fatigue in haemopoietic stem cell transplantation patients', *Journal of Clinical Nursing*, **14**(1), pp. 51–55. Available at: https://doi.org/10.1111/j.1365-2702.2004.00938.x

Kim, S., Park, Y. and Niu, Q. (2017) 'Micro-break activities at work to recover from daily work demands', *Journal of Organizational Behavior*, **38**(1), pp. 28–44.

Kinnunen, U., Feldt, T., de Bloom. J. and Korpela, K. (2015) 'Patterns of daily energy management at work: Relations to employee well-being and job characteristics', *International Archives of Occupational and Environmental Health*, **88**(8), pp. 1077–1086. Available at: https://doi.org/10.1007/s00420-015-1039-9

Kline, N. (2020) *The promise that changes everything: I won't interrupt you.* London: Penguin Random House.

Kniffin, K.M. *et al.*, (2021) 'COVID-19 and the workplace: Implications, issues, and insights for future research and action', *American Psychologist*, **76**(1), pp. 63–77. Available at: https://doi.org/10.1037/amp0000716

Kupriyanov, R. and Zhdanov, R. (2014) 'The eustress concept: Problems and outlooks', *World Journal of Medical Sciences*, **11**(2), pp. 179–185.

Loehr, J. and Schwartz, T. (2003) *The power of full engagement: Managing energy, not time, is the key to high performance and personal renewal.* New York: Free Press.

Loehr, J. (2007) *The power of story: Change your story, change your destiny in business and in life.* New York: Simon and Schuster.

Microsoft (2021) *Research proves your brain needs breaks.* WTI Pulse Report. Available at: http://www.microsoft.com/en-us/worklab/work-trend-index/brain-research#:~:text=In%20our%20latest%20study%20of,a%20simple%20remedy%20E2%80%94short%20breaks

Nakamura, J. and Csikszentmihalyi, M. (2009) 'Flow theory and research'. In Lopez, S.J. and Snyder, C.R. (eds.) *The Oxford handbook of positive psychology*, 2nd edn. Oxford: Oxford University Press, pp. 195–206.

Neff, K.D., Hsieh, Y. and Dejitterat, K. (2005) 'Self-compassion, achievement goals, and coping with academic failure', *Self and Identity*, **4**(3), pp. 263–287.

Neff, K.D. and Pommier, E. (2013) 'The relationship between self-compassion and other-focused concern among college undergraduates, community adults, and practicing meditators', *Self and Identity*, **12**(2), pp. 160–176.

Neil's Wheel (2020) Using the tool – 5 simple steps to get going ... Available at: https://neilswheel.org/using-neils-wheel/

Niessen, C., Sonnentag, S. and Sach, F. (2012) 'Thriving at work: A diary study', *Journal of Organizational Behaviour*, **33**(4), pp. 468–487.

Olsen, O.K., Pallesen, S. and Torsheim, T. and Espevik, R. (2016) 'The effect of sleep deprivation on leadership behaviour in military officers: An experimental study', *Journal of Sleep Research*, **25**(6), pp. 683–689.

Palmer, W. and Crawford, J. (2013) *Leadership embodiment: How the way we sit and stand can change the way we think and speak*. California: Embodiment International.

Parker, S.L., Zacher, H., de Bloom, J., Verton, T.M. and Lentink, C.R. (2017) 'Daily use of energy management strategies and occupational well-being: The Moderating role of job demands', *Frontiers in Psychology*, **8**, pp. 1–12. Available at: https://doi.org/10.3389/fpsyg.2017.01477

Parry, D., Oepen, R.S., Gass, H. and Amin, M.S.A. (2018) 'Sleep: its importance and the effects of deprivation on surgeons and other healthcare professionals', *British Journal of Oral and Maxillofacial Surgery*, **56**, pp. 663–666.

Prentice, K., (2019) *Nature's way: Designing the life you want through the lens of nature and the five seasons*. Karyn Prentice.

Rath, T. (2015) *Are you fully charged? The three keys to energizing your work and life*. US: Missionday.

Riethof, B., Bob, P., Laker, M., Varakova, K., Jiraskova, T. and Raboch, J. (2019) 'Burnout syndrome and logotherapy: Logotherapy as useful conceptual framework for explanation and prevention of burnout', *Frontiers in Psychiatry*, **10**, pp. 1–8. Available at: https://doi.org/10.3389/fpsyt.2019.00382

Rock, D. (2008) 'SCARF: A brain-based model for collaborating with and influencing others', *Neuroleadership Journal*, **1**, pp. 1–9.

Sarner, M. (2021) 'Brain fog: how trauma, uncertainty and isolation have affected our minds and memory', *The Guardian*, 14 April. Available at: https://www.theguardian.com/lifeandstyle/2021/apr/14/brain-fog-how-trauma-uncertainty-andisolation-have-affected-our-minds-and-memory

Schippers, M.C. and Hogenes, R. (2011) 'Energy management of people in organizations: A review and research agenda', *Journal of Business and Psychology*, **26**, pp. 193–203. Available at: https://doi.org/10.1007/s10869-011-9217-6

Schulz, A.S., Bloom, J. and Kinnunen, U. (2017) 'Workaholism and daily energy management at work: Associations with self-reported health and emotional exhaustion', *Industrial Health*, **55**(3), pp. 252–264.

Siegel, D. (2018) *Aware: The science and practice of presence*. London: Scribe Publications.

Spaten, O.M. and Green, S. (2019) 'Delivering value in coaching'. In Passmore, J., Underhill, B.O. and Goldsmith, M. (eds.) *Mastering executive coaching*. Abingdon: Routledge, pp. 90–109.

Spreitzer, G., Sutcliffe, K., Dutton, J., Sonenshein, S. and Grant, A.M. (2005) 'A socially embedded model of thriving at work', *Special Issue: Frontiers of Organization Science*, **16**(5), pp. 537–549.

Swart, T., Chisholm, K. and Brown, P. (2015) *Neuroscience for leadership*. Basingstoke: Palgrave Macmillan.

Thogersen-Ntoumani, C., Loughren, E.A., Kinnafick, F.E., Taylor, I.M., Duda, J.L. and Fox, K.R. (2015) 'Changes in work affect in response to lunchtime walking in previously physically inactive employees: A randomized trial', *Scandinavian Journal of Medicine and Science in Sports*, **25**(6), pp. 778–787.

Trougakos, J.P. and Hideg, I. (2009) 'Momentary work recovery: The role of within-day work breaks'. In Sonnentag, S., Perrewé, P.L. and Ganster, D.C. (eds.) *Current perspectives on job-stress recovery (Research in occupational stress and well-being, Vol 7)*. Bingley: Emerald Publishing Limited, pp. 37–84.

Wasylyshyn, K.M. and Masterpasqua, F. (2018) 'Developing self-compassion in leadership development coaching: A practice model and case study analysis', *International Coaching Psychology Review*, **13**(1), pp. 21–34.

Watkins, A. (2014) *Coherence: The secret science of brilliant leadership*. London: Kogan Page.

Whittington, J. (2020) *Systemic coaching and constellations: The principles, practices and application for individuals, teams and groups*, 3rd edn. London: Kogan Page.

Zacher, H., Brailsford, H.A. and Parker, S.L. (2014) 'Micro-breaks matter: A diary study on the effects of energy management strategies on occupational well-being', *Journal of Vocational Behavior*, **85**(3), pp. 287–297.

Zakerimoghadam, M., Marzieh, S., Anoushiravan, K. and Tavasoli, K.H. (2006) 'The effect of breathing exercises on fatigue level of COPD patients', *Hayat*, **12**(3), pp. 17–25.

Concluding remarks

EXECUTIVE COACHES EXPERIENCE THEIR SENIOR CLIENTS in all sectors working, and pushing themselves, phenomenally hard. Many of our clients do not take the time to think whether they are optimally energised to meet the daily demands made on them and to have positive relationships with those around them in order to be able to live, work and lead in a constructive and healthy way.

In this book I have offered a research-based clarification of the concept of human energy in the context of both the workplace and executive coaching, suggesting that it comes from physical sources and energetic activation, and outlined the many influences on energy which our clients may experience. This will hopefully help coaches recognise energy levels in their clients, consider what influences their client's energy and enable their clients to do this for themselves.

Having optimal, depleted or inappropriate high energy at work will impact a senior executive client's performance, self-awareness, ability to lead and inspire and their relationships with others, sometimes with a considerable ripple effect on the atmosphere in their team or wider organisation. It can also affect their ability to engage with coaching. This book has outlined the array of positive implications of being optimally energised as much as is realistic and possible for an individual. Addressing energy is extremely important because being suboptimally energised presents a risk: poor decisions, behaviour and relationships could be the potential result.

Executive coaches are very well-placed to do this work with our clients. And the observations and recommendations in this book are also relevant to all types of coaches, to coach supervisors and for other practitioners who may want to address energy with their clients in one-to-one and group work. The conscious consideration of personal energy levels and the taking of action, in a sustainable way, will help clients work towards achieving optimal energy, be aware of how it feels when their energy is not optimal and understand the implications. If assessed to be appropriate, coaches can work at so many levels with their clients to address energy: client energy can be acknowledged, enhanced, challenged and nurtured in an executive coaching relationship. Bringing up what we observe with regard to our client's energy levels in sessions may lead to a really interesting conversation in itself. We can give them information about energy, raising awareness of the concept and the influences on it. Clients can, as a result, become more alert to times when they need to act.

This book also outlines what can be done to address energy, how the coach can work with energy within a session and also encourage clients to have their own personal, conscious and proactive approach to managing their energy at a number of levels: in the moment, when they realise that they are getting really tired or are agitated and wired; in order to prepare for a particular event in the future like a meeting or when they realise that their overall performance is being affected. Coaches can do this for themselves too.

Ideally, when senior people within organisations become aware of and are able to act to address their own energy and see how it benefits them, they will help to influence their organisational culture to be one which supports others to do the same, with a senior management team which can take an overall view of, and act to address, significant influences on human energy from an organisational perspective.

Index

Page nos. in *Italics* represent Figures

www.ingramcontent.com/pod-product-compliance
Lightning Source LLC
Chambersburg PA
CBHW070628030426
42337CB00020B/3951